Contents

C000118554

Welcome

1

Welcome!

Welcome to WebPlus X8 from **Serif**—the easiest way to get your business, club, organization, personal interest, or household on the web!

To make life so much easier, WebPlus offers you a simple way to build websites visually, without having to learn or use any traditional web programming. WebPlus comes with an impressive selection of **design templates**, page **navigation bars**, creative **assets**, and **styles** for you to use. Full-size and mobile-friendly templates, along with lots of ready-made content, mean anyone can publish a professional-looking website, no prior experience required! You'll also be able to reuse your existing content by importing word processing documents, images, and many other files.

To make the most of pictures in your site you can use **Cutout Studio** to remove backgrounds and **PhotoLab** for powerful image adjustment and effect combinations. You simply cannot afford to miss them!

WebPlus X8 doesn't just stop at "static" web publishing. The real power comes when adding and managing dynamic or interactive content, such as **forms**, **blogs**, **forums**, **video playlists**, and third-party **RSS feeds.** Also add modern essentials such as **panels**, **sliders**, and **Google Maps**, plus **Facebook**, **Twitter**, and **Google+** widgets. You can even make use of easy **e-commerce tools** with step-by-step setup for shopping cart and donation features.

Once you're happy with your WebPlus site, simply **publish to the web** to share with business colleagues, customers, friends and family alike.

Registration

Don't forget to register your new copy, using the **Registration Wizard**, on the **Help** menu. That way, we can keep you informed of new developments and future upgrades!

This User Guide

The WebPlus X8 User Guide is provided for the new or inexperienced user to get the very best out of WebPlus. As the program is packed with a wealth of features, this User Guide doesn't cover all product functionality, but instead focuses on core and frequently used features. For comprehensive assistance, please use WebPlus Help (press your F1 key).

New features

WebPlus X8 (in 32 and 64-bit versions) introduces even greater ease of use, more design tools, new features for photos, and more advanced editing power.

- **Interactive Task Monitor Tab** (see p. 154)
  The tab acts as a personal design assistant that keeps track of your project and fixes design issues for you. It knows about the state of objects, pages and the site all the time, and can warn about potential problems, remind you to accomplish certain tasks, offer hints, and list issues from the last time a site was published. You can also add your own reminders.

- **Online Resource Manager** (see p. 114)
  Instead of linking large files from your computer and publishing them with your site, the new online resource manager lets you upload media and other files to a remote server. It remembers the addresses of the files, and makes them available when you are choosing resources while designing your site. This allows you to upload once and use repeatedly, and to host large files on a different server from your website without complications.

- **Save as Package**
  Share your WebPlus file or make it easier to move from one computer to another by saving it as a package—a single file that contains your WebPlus site design, the fonts you've used, and any linked images and other resources. Opening the package on another computer will unpack the design and other resources so you can carry on working.

- **Backup to the Web** (see p. 30)
  Protect your site design from hardware failure or accidental deletion by **backing it up to a remote server** at any time (as a regular WebPlus file or Package). Access the new backup command from the File menu at key stages to keep your design safe.

Design and Multimedia

- **Slider Studio** (see p. 68)
  A dedicated **slider design studio** lets you easily configure settings and animation options, add and remove slider panels, and design each panel of the slider. Import images, add text, drag and drop your favourite assets, use graphic design tools to create shapes and apply fills and colours, even apply one-click styles for speedy, consistent design.

- **Scrolling Animations** (see p. 59)
  Two new types of animation give your site a slick and modern feel. Add **Slide on Scroll** to objects as an action, making them appear and disappear from the side of the screen and fade in and out as they are scrolled in or out of view. For longer pages with anchors, set a **smooth scrolling** behaviour to give the site professional polish.

- **Embeddable Fonts**
  Embed fonts with your site to ensure text looks exactly as you intend, without converting fancy styles to images on publishing. A new category of embeddable fonts in the Fonts

tab joins the recently used and websafe categories in your font list, and they can be uploaded with your site for automatic downloading with site content for a better browsing experience.

- **Audio Player** (see p. 120)
  Give visitors an easy way to hear your music and other audio files in your website with a customizable **audio player** that uses the latest HTML5 technology for efficiency and broad compatibility. Add single tracks or entire playlists; the audio player features all the normal controls you'd expect to find including volume and track skipping.

- **New Filter Effects and Settings**
  A new Trail filter effect gives logos and other designs a striking retro style, and new options allow fine tuning of feathering, drop shadows and other effects.

- **New photo editing tools and effects**
  Vibrance, Split Tone, Tilt Shift, and Clarity PhotoLab filters add fantastic effects to enhance pictures, plus new tools offer selective editing and photo repair. Now control vignette positioning and sizing. Blend effects smoothly across an area using gradient masks, and remove unwanted blemishes, clutter or imperfections with a clone brush.

Photo Tools

- **Pin it!** (see p. 40)
  Add an interactive 'Pin it' button to share photos on **Pinterest**, the popular image interest service. The button appears when the image is hovered over and is easily added in WebPlus **as an action**.

- **Image Watermarking** (see p. 39)
  Protect original photography, artwork and other valuable images by adding a watermark. Once you design a watermark it can be incorporated into images when you publish your site

and does not modify original photo files. Choose text or a logo, set transparency, size, tiling and other options, and see a preview of your watermark while you design it.

- **Magnifier** (see p. 39)
  Set an area on your page to show a magnified image, with settings for zoom controls and mouse wheel operation. Optionally set the image extent as the magnifier area, so visitors can zoom and pan around inside an image without requiring extra page space.

- **Galleries in Date Order** (see p. 69)
  WebPlus **photo galleries** now offer a way for photos to be displayed in order by date taken, so you can more easily tell a story with a sequence of pictures.

- **Quick Image Optimization**
  Images can be optimized automatically when you publish your site, and there's also a new way to select multiple images and scale them to the size at which they are used in the site, in one go, in the Resource Manager.

Interactivity and Output

- **New Site Search** (see p. 88)
  An improved **site search** feature indexes content from blogs, forums and other Smart Objects in addition to regular website content. Tags can be added to pages to help categorize and fine tune site search results to just those pages.

- **New User Management Controls** (see p. 99)
  User accounts now have a new site membership control to join the existing mailing list signup and website login controls. The site membership control offers access to profiles, avatars, screen names, passwords and list subscriptions.

- **Custom CSS and HTML Attributes**
  Attach custom HTML attributes and custom CSS properties to objects, without converting the object to code and without entering the code editing view. Simply add the new attributes via the object's Properties dialog.

- **Export as Widget**
  Output interactive elements of your websites as widgets that can be incorporated into other websites, whether hand coding or using other web design software. Navigation bars, popup menus, photo galleries, sliders and many other WebPlus designed features can be exported, including the necessary HTML, scripts and graphics files.

- **SFTP Secure File Transfer** (see p. 157)
  Enable SFTP for secure file transfer and secure file management when **publishing** and connecting to remote servers, if the protocol is supported by the server.

Installation

Installing WebPlus follows different procedures depending on whether you are installing from disc or via download.

> You can install your new version alongside previous versions and use them independently.

> 32 or 64-bit WebPlus X8 installs to respective 32 or 64-bit computers.

Installation procedure (from disc)

- Insert your purchased disc into your disc drive.

    - If AutoPlay is enabled on the drive, this automatically starts the Setup Wizard. Follow the on-screen instructions for install.

    -or-

    - If AutoPlay is not enabled (or doesn't start the install automatically), navigate to your program disc and double-click **autorun.exe**.

Installation procedure (from download)

- From **serif.com**, when logged into your Serif account, follow the on-screen instructions to download.

System Requirements

Minimum:

- Windows-based PC* with mouse or equivalent input device

- Operating systems:
  Windows® 8 (32 or 64 bit)
  Windows® 7 (32 or 64 bit)
  Windows® Vista (32 or 64 bit)
  Microsoft Windows® XP SP3 (32 bit)

- PC Memory:
  512MB RAM (Windows® XP)
  1GB RAM (Windows® Vista and 32-bit Windows 7® and 8)
  2GB RAM (For 64-bit Windows® 7 and 8)

- Hard Drive Space:
  281MB free hard disk space for physical media install (and a DVD drive)
  396MB free hard disk space for download install (additional space required during installation)

- 1024 x 768 monitor resolution (at 100% scaling)
  1280 x 960 monitor resolution (at 125% scaling)
  1536 x 1152 monitor resolution (at 150% scaling)
  2048 x 1536 monitor resolution (at 200% scaling)

- Other:
  Internet Explorer 9
  Internet account and connection required for publishing to web and accessing online resources
  * Main processor must support SSE2 instructions.

Additional disk resources and memory are required when editing large and/or complex sites.

Optional:

- Windows-compatible printer

- TWAIN-compatible scanner and/or digital camera

- .NET 2.0 for text import filters (Word 2007/2010 +
  OpenOffice) (installed by default; for Windows 8, an extra 1GB
  of free hard disk space is required)

Setting up Sites and Pages

2

Startup Assistant

Once WebPlus has been installed, you're ready to start.

- For Windows Vista/7: Setup adds a **Serif WebPlus X8** item to the **All Programs** submenu of the Windows **Start** menu. Use the Windows **Start** button to pop up the Start menu, click on **All Programs** and then click **Serif WebPlus X8**.

- For Windows 8: The Setup routine during install adds a **Serif WebPlus X8** entry to the desktop and also to the Start screen. Double-click the WebPlus icon from the desktop, or click the WebPlus tile on the Start screen.

On program launch, the Startup Assistant is displayed which offers different routes into WebPlus:

The options are described as follows:

The default home page keeps you in touch with Serif promotions and showcases articles (tutorials, etc.) You can also view the WebPlus Overview and Quick Start video.

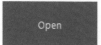
To access WebPlus files; also provides recent file history.

For online video/written tutorials, help, tips & tricks, and more—all via an updating feed that can be filtered by article Type. The Product Help and your electronic WebPlus X8 user guide are also provided.

Creates a new website from scratch, using a simple setup.

Creates an instant website from a pre-designed template.

For cross-product news, company news, articles, and product announcements, using Serif's news feed.

Any time you access the Startup Assistant, the Learn or News buttons indicate the number of new articles to be viewed (if available). This number will decrease as you read each article in the Learn or News pane. When new articles arrive, these will be indicated the next time you open the Startup Assistant.

 To access the Startup Assistant when WebPlus is already running, choose Startup Assistant from the File menu.

Creating a site using a design template

WebPlus comes complete with a whole range of categorized design templates which will speed you through the creation of all kinds of websites.

Each template offers:

- **Complementary design**—Professionally designed layout with high-visual impact.

- **Schemes**—choose a named colour scheme to apply a specific look and feel.

- **Page selection**—select some or all template pages (e.g., Home, Products, About Us, etc.) to base your new site on.

Design templates come in two types—**theme layouts** and ready-to-go **Pro templates**.

Theme layouts

These offer a choice of themes (e.g., Eco, Pop, Prospectus, and many more) on which to base your site. Simply add your own pictures to placeholders and personalize placeholder titles and text, then publish.

Ready-to-go Pro templates
These are categorized templates containing royalty-free pictures and catchy titles which can be adopted to fast-track you to your completed website. You just need to personalize placeholder text, and then publish.

Equivalent mobile-ready layouts are available for both theme layouts and Pro templates—these can be used to create your own site optimized for smart phone access.

To create a site using a design template:

1. Open WebPlus, or select **Startup Assistant** from the **File** menu.

2. Click **Templates**.

3. From the Templates pane, select a desktop or mobile option from Theme Layouts or WebPlus X8 Pro Templates categories.

4. Navigate the main pane by scrolling using the right-hand scroll bar.

5. Select a thumbnail design you like from the main pane.

Theme Layout (Desktop)   *Theme Layout (Mobile)*

Pro Design Template (Desktop)   *Pro Design Template (Mobile)*

6. From the right-hand pane, decide which pages you wish to be part of your site. Check or uncheck under each page to select or deselect, respectively.

7. Pick a **Colour Scheme** from the drop-down list at the top of the dialog (the first three schemes are designed specifically for the chosen template). With the drop-down list open, you can preview your pages as you scroll through the schemes by using your keyboard up/down arrow keys. The page thumbnails will refresh to reflect the new page's appearance.

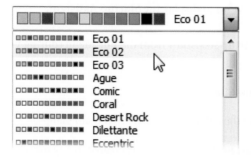

8. (Optional) Use the BACK button if you want to alter your choices.

9. Click **OK**. The pages are added to your new site.

Starting a site from scratch

Although **design templates** (p. 14) can simplify your design choices, you
can just as easily start out from scratch with a new, blank site. Your site
is created via the **Startup Assistant** which helps cover the key aspects of
your site's creation.

To start a new site from scratch (via Startup Assistant):

1. Open WebPlus to display the **Startup Assistant**.
    - or -
    Select **Startup Assistant** from the **File** menu (during your
    session).

2. Select **New Site**.

3. Complete the details in the displayed main pane.

4. Click **Start new site**. Your site is created, ready for editing.

At this stage and subsequently, Site Properties can be edited to fine-tune
your site settings. Select **Site Properties** via the **Properties** menu.

> From the Startup Assistant, you can press the **Esc** key to open a
> blank publication using default page properties.

To start a new blank site during your WebPlus session:

- During your WebPlus session, click  **New Site** on the **Standard** toolbar.

The new site opens with a blank page using default **site properties**.

Opening an existing site

You can open an existing WebPlus site from the **Startup Assistant**, **Standard** toolbar, or via the **File** menu.

To open an existing publication (via Startup Assistant):

1. Open WebPlus to display the initial **Startup Assistant**.
   - or -
   Select **Startup Assistant** from the **File** menu (during your session).

2. Select **Open**.

3. Several options are possible:

   i. For recently opened sites, select a thumbnail from the main pane.

Today

mywebsite.wpp

ii.   The site opens in your workspace.

- or -

i.   For other WebPlus sites, select **WebPlus files** from the
      Browse My Computer pane.

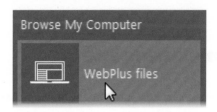

ii.   From the dialog, locate and select your file, then click
       Open.

Understanding site structure

The "structure" of a website has nothing to do with its physical layout, or
where pages are stored. Rather, it's a way of logically arranging the
content on the site so that visitors have an easier time navigating
through it. One of the most useful organizing principles—which
WebPlus strongly reinforces—is an "inverted tree" structure that starts
with the Home page and then branches out to other pages. To the visitor
navigating your site, this arrangement presents your content in a
familiar, hierarchical way, structured into **sections** and **levels**.

- A **section** is a content category, each being a separate page, e.g.
  "Home, "About Us", "Gallery", "Products", and "Contact".

- The **level** is the number of steps (i.e., jumps) a given page is
  removed from its "parent" page. The Home page will always
  reside at Level 1, normally along with "section" pages. This
  allows navigation bars to work easily and automatically. Pages

one step below the "section" pages reside at Level 2, and are considered to be child pages of the "parent" page.

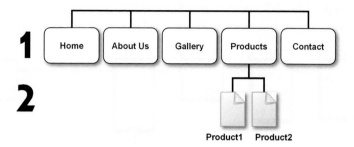

Viewing site structure

Two ways of viewing the site structure are possible: via the **Pages** tab or via the **Site Structure View**. The latter is ideal for viewing larger sites.

Via Pages tab

In WebPlus, the Site Structure tree (in the Pages tab) provides a visual aid that lets you organize the content on your site into sections and levels. Here's how the above structure might appear:

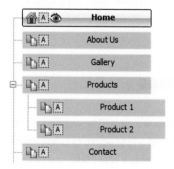

Via Site Structure View

For larger websites, **Site Structure view** can be used instead of the Pages tab to provide a full-screen display that previews your "section and level" site structure as page thumbnails presented in a tree-based structure.

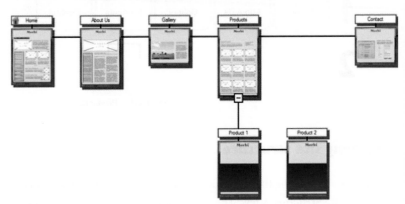

To view your site structure:

- From the **Standard** toolbar, select **View Site Structure**.

The toolbar also lets you show and preview pages, include/exclude pages in navigation, rearrange pages by drag-and-drop, and even Quick Publish the selected page(s).

Setting site properties

Site properties allow settings to be made which will be applied across the entire site. Generally speaking, important site properties (page width, height, etc. are automatically set on selecting a **template** or when **starting from scratch**. Other settings do not normally need to be modified (although you can at any time).

Some site properties such as page appearance and search-engine optimization settings are also mirrored on individual pages (via **Page Properties**). This lets you override or complement the "global" Site Properties, respectively, and apply "local" settings to specific pages.

To view or change site property settings:

- Select ⊞ **Site Properties** from the default context toolbar.
  - or -

  Choose **Site Properties** from the **Properties** menu.

Understanding pages and master pages

Looking at individual pages from a design standpoint, each WebPlus page has a "foreground" **page** and a "background" **master page**.

Master pages provide a flexible way to store background elements that you would like to appear on more than one page—for example a logo, background, header/footer, border design, or navigation bar.

The key concept here is that a particular master page is typically shared by multiple pages, as illustrated below. By placing a design element on a master page and then assigning several pages to use that master page, you ensure that all the pages incorporate that element. Of course, each individual page can have its own elements.

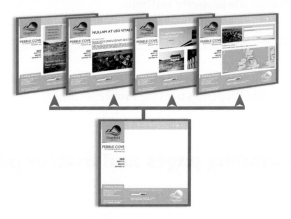

The **Pages** tab includes an upper Master Pages section containing your master page(s), and a lower Site Structure in the Pages window containing your standard pages. Each page shown in the window indicates the master page being used for that page.

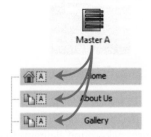

For more varied page designs across your site, you can **create** more than one master page (see p. 26).

Once you have multiple master pages, they can be **attached to separate pages** or **in combination on the same page**.

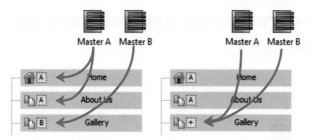

Attaching different master pages

By default, pages created in new sites have a master page (e.g., Master A) automatically attached to them. However, if your site has more than one master page you can attach a different master page to the page instead.

To attach a different master page to a page:

1. In the Pages tab, right-click the page and select **Page Properties**.

2. From the dialog's Master Pages menu option, uncheck the original master page, then check the master page you want to use.

3. Click **OK**.

To detach a master page:

- Uncheck its entry in the Page Properties dialog (Master Page menu option).

> Unchecking all master pages means that the page will use the site appearance **(Properties>Site Properties)**.

Adding, removing, and rearranging pages

Using the **Pages** tab, you can:

- **Add** and d**elete** pages.

- Add one or more **master pages**.

- Use drag-and-drop to **rearrange** pages.

- Add pages from installed design **templates**.

- Add **offsite links**.

- Add **HTML pages**.

- Set a page to be the **home page**.

Use the upper Master Pages window of the Pages tab to access master pages, and the Pages window (tab's central Site Structure tree) to access pages.

Besides the Pages tab, WebPlus offers a variety of other ways to manipulate pages:

- **Site Structure View** for a tree view of your site as page thumbnails, with supporting page manipulation.

- **Master Page Manager** for adding and copying master pages, as well as controlling multiple master pages.

Adding pages

To add a new blank page:

1.   In the Pages Window of the Pages tab, select a page after which you want to add the new page.

2.   Click the down arrow on the  **Add** button directly above the Pages tab's Pages window. From the drop-down menu, choose **New Blank Page**.

3.   In the Page Properties dialog, specify options for the new page from each of the menu options in turn.

4.   Click **OK**.

A new page appears at the specified location in the site structure.

> Any new page created will use the currently set **Site Properties** (**Properties** menu), such as the default page size and alignment, but you can overwrite site properties by editing **Page Properties**.

Adding master pages

To add a new master page:

1.   On the **Pages** tab, ensure the **Master Pages>** button is clicked to expand the Master Page Window.

2.   Click the  **Add** button above the Master Pages window.

A new master page appears in the Pages tab's Master Pages window.

To reassign pages to particular master pages, see **Understanding pages and master pages** on p. 23.

Deleting pages

To delete a page or master page:

1. On the Pages tab, select the page (or master page) to delete by clicking its entry.

2. Click **Delete selected page** above the appropriate window to delete the page.

Creating HTML pages

HTML pages can be added to any Pages tab's Site Structure. Such pages are included in navigation as standard pages. See Creating HTML pages in WebPlus Help for more information.

Rearranging pages

Besides using the Pages tab to add or delete pages, you can use it to rearrange pages as needed.

To move a page:

1. Display the **Pages** tab.

2. Click to select the page in the Site Structure tree.

3. (Using drag-and-drop) Drag the page entry up or down and drop it at a new position in the tree. Watch the cursor for feedback on the new position relative to that of the page just below the cursor:

 moves the page to the same level as, and following, the highlighted target page.

 makes the page a child of the page below the highlighted target page.

Adding template pages

While adding a blank page gives you page design freedom, you can make life a little easier by adopting "ready to go" template pages. You can select template pages that complement your existing theme layout or choose an independent template page.

This is possible by selecting **New Template Page** on the **Pages** tab's **Add new page or link** drop-down list.

Adding offsite links

You can also add an **offsite link** to your site structure. Typically, this would be a page (blog or forum) or resource separate from your site that you wanted to include in your site's navigation structure. The offsite link appears in the Site Structure tree and in navigation bars, so you can manipulate it just as if it were a page in your site.

The **New Offsite Link** on the **Pages** tab's **Add new page or link** drop-down list allows you to do this.

Setting your home page

To make a web page your home page:

- Right-click on a standard page in your Pages tab then select **Set as Home Page**.

Setting page properties

Your WebPlus site has its own general framework, consisting of the **site** itself; one or more **master pages**; and a number of individual **pages**. Each aspect of the framework has various **property** settings that contribute to the look and behaviour or your site when it's published. Whether you start with a WebPlus template or from scratch, you can choose whether to stick with the default property settings or alter them to suit your needs.

To view or change page (master page) property settings:

- Select **Page Properties** from the default context toolbar.
  - or -
  Right-click the active page and select **Page Properties**.

Backing up your site to web

You can save your WebPlus project file (.wpp) with fonts and linked resources to back it up in your website hosting location, or to somewhere else if you want. This guards against accidental deletion or something inadvertently happening to the computer that was used to create the site. Additionally, you can backup as a package. See WebPlus Help.

To Back up to site:

1. Save your site in WebPlus.

2. From the **File** menu, select **Backup Site to Web**.

    If you attempt to backup your site without configuring your
    FTP account settings first, a dialog appears. You'll be able to
    add existing FTP account details as described in Quick Publish.

The **Backup To web** dialog displays. The hosting location where
your site is about to backed up to is shown in the **Publishing to**
field.

3. To backup your site to a different hosting location, click
    Change and update account settings, or add a new account.

4. Check **Backup as a package** if required.

5. Click **OK**. The File Operation dialog displays the progress of
    the backup.

6. Click **OK.**

Restore your web site

1. Click the  **Publish site** flyout on the **Standard** toolbar
    and then click **Maintain Web Site**.
    - or-

From the **File** menu, select **Publish Site** and then choose
Maintain Web Site from the submenu.

The **Maintain Website** dialog appears.

2. Select your FTP account name (from the drop-down list) and
    type in your **Password** (if not saved).

3. Click **Maintain**.
    WebPlus seeks an Internet connection and displays a dialog
    showing the navigable website's folders in the left-hand window
    and any selected folder's contents in the adjacent window.

4. In the adjacent window, click to select the WebPlus project file
    and click **Download from Server** from the buttons above.

5. From the dialog, select a location on your computer to save the
    file locally.

6. Click the window's **Close** button to terminate the FTP
    connection and return to WebPlus.

Layout Items

3

Inserting text frames

Typically, text in WebPlus goes into **text frames**, which work equally well as containers for single words or standalone paragraphs and articles. You can also use **artistic text** (see p. 137) for standalone text with special effects, or **table text** (see **Inserting tables** on p. 45) for row-and-column displays.

Creating text frames

You add frames to a page as you would any other object.

> You can select, move, and resize any frame, but you cannot alter its basic shape. (See WebPlus Help for more information.)

> When you resize a text frame, its story text reflows to the new dimensions.

To create a frame:

1. On the Quick Build tab (Layout Items category), click **Text Frame**.

2. Drag out to place the text frame at your chosen dimensions.
   - or -

   Click on the page or pasteboard to create a new frame at a default size.

Putting text into a frame

You can put text into a frame in one of several ways.

WritePlus story editor:	With a selected frame, click **WritePlus** on the Frame context toolbar.
Importing text:	Right-click on a frame and choose **Insert>Text File** to import text.
Typing into the frame:	Select the Pointer Tool, then click for an insertion point to type text straight into a frame, or edit existing text. (See **Editing text on the page** on p. 139.)
Pasting via the Clipboard:	At an insertion point in the text, press **Ctrl+V**.

Controlling overflowing frame text

Fitting story text precisely into text frames is part of the art of laying out websites. If there's too much story text to fit in your text frame, WebPlus stores it in an **overflow area** hidden from view (but not lost!) at the bottom of the frame.

The **Text overflow** button displays under the overflowing frame to indicate this hidden text, so it's important to ensure the text is made to display again, otherwise your story will remain truncated.

To do this, several options are open to you:

- Physically resize your text frame if you have space.

- Consider rewriting your story, making it more concise!

- Resize your text, as described below.

To resize frame text once frames are sized and positioned, various text sizing and AutoFit options are available on the Frame context toolbar.

Inserting pictures

The **Assets** tab (Pictures category) acts as a "basket" for initially gathering together and then including pictures in your site. Its chief use is to aid the design process by improving efficiency (avoiding having to import pictures one by one) and convenience.

WebPlus also lets you **insert pictures** from the **Quick Build** tab or **Basic** toolbar.

Adding pictures to the Assets tab

To add pictures to the tab:

1.   Select the **Assets** tab's Pictures category, and click **Add**.

2.   From the dialog, navigate to a folder, and select your picture(s).

3.   Click **Open**. Your pictures appear as thumbnails within the **Assets** tab's Pictures category.

To reorder pictures in the tab:

- Select and drag a picture to a new position in the tab.

To delete a picture from the tab:

- Right-click a picture and select **Delete Asset**.

Adding pictures to the page

Pictures can be added to your site by dragging directly onto your page.

To add a picture to your page:

- From the **Assets** tab (Pictures category), drag a picture thumbnail directly onto the page, inline into artistic/frame text (at a chosen insertion point), or into a placeholder/populated picture frame.

Once added, the picture thumbnail indicates the number of times the picture has been used in the site (①).

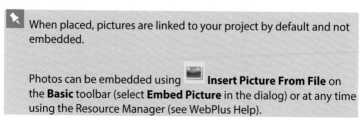

When placed, pictures are linked to your project by default and not embedded.

Photos can be embedded using ▨ **Insert Picture From File** on the **Basic** toolbar (select **Embed Picture** in the dialog) or at any time using the Resource Manager (see WebPlus Help).

Replacing pictures

You can swap a picture at any time, especially useful when you want to retain the position and dimensions on the page but want to update the picture itself. It can be used on any image (uncropped or cropped).

To replace a picture:

1. Click **Replace Picture from File** or **Replace Picture from Assets** directly under the selected picture. This sources pictures from anywhere on your computer or from a supplied (or custom) Asset Pack, respectively.

2. Use the **Import Picture** dialog to select the picture to open.

3. Click **Open**.

You can also replace a picture with those stored in the Asset Browser—click **Replace Picture from Assets** directly under the selected picture.

Displaying pictures in lightboxes

Lightboxes are a simple way of displaying pop-up larger sized versions of pictures from thumbnails you add to your web page. A great advantage of lightboxes is that bigger pictures can be displayed on demand and are superimposed over your web page after a gliding animation.

To create a lightbox for a picture on your web page:

1. Select the picture (preferably a thumbnail).

2. Create a **hyperlink** to it (click **Hyperlink** from the **Properties** menu).

3. Select **Picture** from the menu, then from the **Target Window** tab, choose **Lightbox** from the **Type** drop-down list.

Displaying pictures using Picture Magnifier

Picture Magnifier lets you hover over areas of your picture for an overlaid or offset magnified view. This is done by applying an action called "Magnifier" by double-clicking the picture, selecting the Actions tab and adding the Magnifier action.

Watermarking pictures

If you want to indicate ownership or copyright of your pictures you can apply preset or custom watermarks to individual and multiple pictures (on page or across site) via the Picture context toolbar.

Sharing via Pinterest

Any picture in your site can be shared via the picture-based social media website Pinterest. This is done by applying a Pinterest **action** to the picture by double-clicking the picture, selecting the Actions tab, and clicking Add to add the Pinterest action.

Cutting out pictures

Cutout Studio offers a powerful integrated solution for cutting objects out from their backgrounds. Depending on the make up of your pictures you can separate subject of interests from their backgrounds, either by retaining the subject of interest (usually people, objects, etc.) or removing a simple uniform background (e.g., sky, studio backdrop). In both instances, the resulting "cutout" image creates an eye-catching look for your site.

To launch Cutout Studio:

1. Select an image to be cut out.

2. Select **Cutout Studio** from the displayed Picture context toolbar. Cutout Studio is launched.

3. Click either ![Keep brush icon] **Keep brush** or ![Discard brush icon] **Discard brush** from the left of the Studio workspace, and paint regions to be kept or discarded. Follow the Help pane in the studio for more detailed information.

Picture adjustments and effects

PhotoLab is a powerful studio for applying adjustment and effect filters to pictures, either individually or in combination!

(A) main toolbar, (B) main workspace, (C) filter stack, (D) filter tabs, (E) Images tab

To launch PhotoLab:

1. Select the picture that you want to apply a filter to.

2. Click ![PhotoLab icon] **PhotoLab** on the Picture context toolbar.

3. Select a filter from the filter tabs (Favourites, Adjustments, or Effects).

4. Adjust the filter's settings to your liking in the lower-right **Trial Zone**, then click **Commit**.

5. Repeat for additional filters.

6. Click **OK**.

For more information, see WebPlus Help.

CSS Properties

You can also control the border, padding, outline, background images and visibility of your object by adjusting its CSS properties.

CSS properties are stored efficiently as code rather than being created as part of your graphics, and are applied dynamically by visitors' web browsers. For more information, see CSS properties in WebPlus Help.

Inserting panels

Panels are information boxes superimposed over your web page, which can host pictures and text (below), as well as shapes and line art.

The ability to superimpose panels means that you can increase the amount of information available to the web visitor without altering the underlying web page content. Panels can also be made to display only when required as you click or roll over **buttons**, pictures, or other **assets**. They can also be made to display permanently—great for navigation bars that never disappear on window scrolling!

Panels are also used as building blocks for creating animated **sliders** (p. 66). Like revolving advertising hoardings around sports stadiums, sliders can be made to change which panel is displayed at set time intervals.

Inserting your panel

To insert a panel:

1. From the Quick Build tab (Layout Items), click ☐ **Panel**.

2. Drag the cursor across your page to define the size and shape of your panel region.

The **Insert Panel** dialog opens.

3. In the **Panel** tab:

 • Click the panel preview box.

Transparent

- In the **Asset Browser**, select a panel background design and click **OK**.

  The preview box updates with your chosen panel design.

4. Click **OK**.

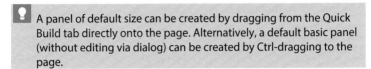
A panel of default size can be created by dragging from the Quick Build tab directly onto the page. Alternatively, a default basic panel (without editing via dialog) can be created by Ctrl-dragging to the page.

To edit a panel:

- Double-click the panel and edit the panel settings.

Adding content to your panel

You should treat your panel as an empty building block which can be developed using WebPlus standard tools and features. By creating objects within the panel area, they belong to the panel. This extends to objects such as text frames, artistic text, tables, QuickShapes, and pictures. Dragging the panel will also move its associated objects.

Hiding/showing your panel

If you've placed a panel on the page, it can be hidden by default, and then displayed only on hover over.

To hide/show a panel:

1. Select the panel.

2. From the context toolbar, select ⚙ **Actions**. The **Edit Panel** dialog opens, displaying the **Actions** tab.

3. Click **Add** and choose **Visibility** from the flyout.

4.   Select the panel from the **Object ID** drop-down list.

5.   Select an event from the **Event** drop-down list.

The event relates to the behaviour that occurs when you perform an action (i.e., when you click or rollover the object).

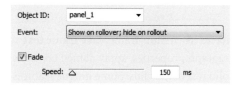

6.   Click **OK**.

Finally, the panel can be hidden with a single click once you've finished designing it.

To hide a selected panel:

•   From the context toolbar, select **Show or Hide the object**.

> To toggle the visibility of hidden objects as you design, from the
> **View** menu, select **Hidden Objects**.

On publishing your page, a rollover of the panel will display it.

It's possible to create custom panel backgrounds by using WebPlus's Design Studio. See WebPlus help for more information.

Inserting tables

Tables are ideal for presenting text and data in a variety of easily customizable row-and-column formats, with built-in spreadsheet capabilities.

			£/€
Vivamus vel	345-56	1	4.24/4.97
Praesent nisl	334-B299	2	4.64/5.44
Mauris nibh	089-78	2	2.93/3.44
Nullam eleifend	455-13	1	7.10/8.32
Donec viverra	345-33	1	2.55/2.99

Each cell in a table behaves like a mini-frame. Like **frame text** you can vary character and paragraph properties, apply named text styles, embed inline images, apply solid text colour fills. Some unique features include number formatting and formula insertion.

To insert a table:

1. From the Quick Build tab (Layout Items), click ⊞ **Table**.

2. Click on your page, or drag out to set the size of your table.

    The **Create Table** dialog appears with a selection of preset table formats shown in the **Format** window.

3. Step through the list to preview the layouts and select one (use up/down keyboard arrows for a "live" preview of each). To begin with a plain table, select **(Default)**.

4. (Optional) Click **Edit** if you want to further customize your chosen format.

5. Set the **Table Size**. This is the number of rows and columns that make up the table layout.

6. Click **OK**. The new table appears on the page.

To modify the structure and cell contents of tables, please see Manipulating tables in WebPlus Help.

Navigation Items

4

Inserting navigation bars

Navigation bars are used to allow the site visitor to jump between pages serving different purposes, e.g. Home page, Gallery, Products, and Contact Us. They are automatically programmed to understand your **site structure** (see p. 20), making it easy to design a site that's simple to navigate.

Technically, navigation bars facilitate movement between the various **sections and levels** of a site (see p. 20), providing links to your Home page and other top-level section pages, while pop-up menus link to child pages within each section.

You can easily install navigation bars at any level of your site, reconfigure them to link to a particular part of the site, change the appearance of the navigation bar, and exclude particular pages from navigation as needed.

Inserting navigation bars

Navigation bars can be added to any page but are typically added to the **master page**—as this saves you the trouble of pasting the same element to multiple pages.

When inserting a navigation bar, you can choose how your navigation will appear on your page by choosing:

- **Type**: The intrinsic design of your navigation bar (e.g., designer, graphical, simple).

- **Navigation Type**: The site or custom structure on which the navigation bar is based.

- **Appearance**: The button, separator, and background design of the navigation bar. Either preset or custom designs can be used.

- **Pop-Up Menus**: The design of the text-based or button-based pop-up menu displaying off the navigation bar (if using child pages in your site structure).

- **ID/Anchor**: The HTML ID for the navbar object and the object's anchor can be set.

- **CSS Properties**: Some navigation bars can have CSS styling applied, e.g. a border. See CSS properties in WebPlus Help.

- **Actions**: An action (change in Z-order, opacity, or custom) can be applied as a result of an event (mouse over). See **Applying actions** on p. 59.

To insert a navigation bar:

1. Select the page (or master page).

2. From the **Quick Build** tab (Navigation Items), click **Navigation Bar**.

3. Position your cursor and click at the point where you want your navigation bar to be placed (the bar will be aligned to the right of this point).

4. From the dialog's **Type** tab, browse navigation bar categories, clicking ⊞ to expand if necessary.

5. Review each navigation bar in turn (or scroll through the bars using the keyboard arrows for quick browsing)! Select your chosen navigation type, e.g. Tabs 2.

    - or -

    Click the **Browse Assets...** button to see previews of all navigation bars in the asset browser. Select an item and click **OK** to return to the dialog.

6. From the **Navigation Type** tab choose whether to base your navigation bar directly on the site's **Site Structure** (enable **Based on site structure**)—an example site structure taken from the program's Pages tab is shown below.

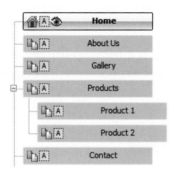

    - or -

    Customize the navigation bar's options (enable **Custom**).

    If choosing **Based on site structure**, you can:

*   Select the level of pages that will be included in the navigation bar: **Top Level**, **Parent Level**, **Same Level**, etc.

- Depending on the main selection, you can opt to include the **child pages**, **anchors**, **home page**, **parent page,** and/or **Hide current page** or **disabled links**.

From the **Advanced** option, set target frame/window, page ordering, and relative links:

7. Click **OK**. The navigation bar appears on your page.

Tips:

- Some navigation bars are colour schemed, allowing further control of the bar's appearance.

- Use the Task Monitor tab to add navigation-related tasks and reminders.

To edit a navigation bar:

1. Double-click the navigation bar.

2. Change settings available from each tab as described above.

It's also possible to customize navigation bars, buttons, separators, and backgrounds for your own navigation bar styles. See WebPlus Help.

Inserting pop-up menus

Pop-up menus form an integral part of multi-level **navigation bars** (p. 48), showing as menus that display only on button hover over. The items in pop-up menus represent child pages at lower levels of your site.

You can also add pop-up menus to any object (a QuickShape, image, a gallery item, but most typically a **button**), the menu being essentially the same as those integrated with navigation bars. Like navigation bars, the pop-up menu items that display can be configured, either adopting the entire site structure, just part of it, or your own custom structure.

You have full control of what level of your site you want to present in the pop-up menu. In the example opposite, the pop-up menu is based on child pages belonging to a Products parent page (which would probably host the button and pop-up menu).

To create a pop-up menu:

1. Select an object to attach the pop-up menu to.

2. From the **Properties** menu, select **Pop-Up Menu**.
    - or -

    Right-click an object and select **Pop-Up Menu**.

3. From the dialog's **Navigation Type** tab, check the **Show a pop-up menu of navigation links for this object** option to enable navigation from this object.

4. Enable **Based on site structure** or **Custom** to either use your site's navigation links as part of the menu or base the pop-up menu on your own **custom structure**, respectively. With the former, you can base your menu on child pages of a top-level "Products" page.

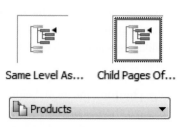

5. From the dialog's **Menu Appearance** tab, select **Text pop-up menus** or **Graphical pop-up menus**. The latter implements button objects to make up its menus.

6. Select a menu option from the box, then edit the values in input boxes, the choices in drop-down lists, select radio buttons, and check boxes to alter your pop-up menu design. Graphical pop-up menu settings for buttons, separators, and background share similar settings to those of **buttons**.

7. Click **OK**.

Inserting buttons

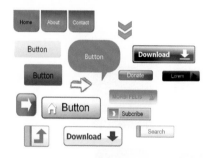

Buttons are an integral part of WebPlus **navigation bars** (see p. 48) but can also be added onto your web page, either standalone or as part of a form. When clicked by the web visitor, they can be made to display a **hyperlink destination**, **pop-up menu**, or trigger an **action**.

In WebPlus, buttons can be either a **preset design** or be **created from scratch** in the **Button Studio**. It's quite common to choose a preset and then customize it to fit your requirements (e.g., change the label text or its colour).

To insert a preset button:

1. From the Quick Build tab (Navigation Items category), click  **Button**.

2. Position your cursor and click at the point where you want your button to be placed. Alternatively, to set the size of the button, drag out a region and release the mouse button.

3. From the **Insert Button** dialog, click the button preview box.

4. From the **Asset Browser**, select a preset button type and click **OK**.

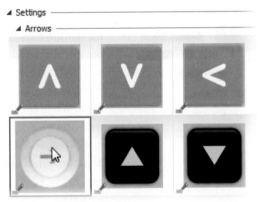

The preview box updates with your chosen button design.

5. Enter a **Button Label** to identify the button, such as "Home", "Images", "Help", etc. (available only for buttons that allow a text label).

6. From the Hyperlink tab:

- From the Hyperlink Type tab, select a link destination type which will direct the user to a target (e.g., Internet page, site page, file) via a **hyperlink** (see p. 57).

- From the Target Window tab, select a window or frame type from the Type drop-down list. For example, you could open the target page in a "New Window".

7. Click **OK**.

Additional tabs, called **Advanced** (Hyperlink tab) and **Actions**, offer accessibility and search engine relationship (REL) attributes, and a range of **actions** (p. 59) that can control user interactivity with your button. **ID/ Anchor** and **CSS Properties** tabs offer advanced controls and styling options.

For a range of website buttons and other graphical elements stored in Asset Packs, you can use the **Asset Browser**. From the **Assets** tab, click **Browse**, then select the Settings category.

To edit a button:

- Double-click a button and edit as described above.

Creating custom buttons

If you're looking to further modify your chosen button preset (or work from scratch) you can use **Button Studio**, a button design environment integrated into WebPlus. This allows you to focus on your button design without the distractions of other objects on the page, i.e. the design is displayed in isolation.

See WebPlus Help for more information.

To edit a button design:

- Select [icon] **Edit Button Design** from the context toolbar.

Adding hyperlinks and actions

Hyperlinking an object such as a box, some text, or a picture means that a visitor to your website can click on the object to trigger an event. The event is most commonly a jump to one of the following hyperlink targets:

- **Site page**

- **Internet page** (somewhere on the web)

- **Internet Email**

- **Anchor** (a designated target within a web page)

- **File on your local disk or network** (for download of files)

- **Shopping cart**

- **Smart object** (e.g., a forum, blog or CMS)

- **RSS feed** (or podcast)

- **Navigation element**

- **User Data**

- **Picture**

Actions are conceptually like hyperlinks, in that something happens on object click or rollover. They differ from hyperlinks in that a click or rollover produces an on-page user interaction with the object, rather than take you to a target destination. (See **Applying actions** on p. 59.)

Adding hyperlinks

To add a hyperlink:

1. Use the **Pointer Tool** to select the single or grouped object or highlight the region of text to be hyperlinked.

2. Select **Hyperlink** from the **Properties** toolbar.

   The object's properties dialog appears.

3. On the **Hyperlink Type** tab (**Hyperlink** tab), click to select the link destination type, i.e. a Site Page, Internet Page, Smart Object, etc.

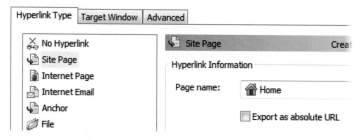

4. Depending on the link type, choose type-specific options in the right-hand pane.

5. Click **OK**.

To modify or remove a hyperlink:

1. Use the **Pointer Tool** to select the object, or click for an insertion point inside the linked text. (It's not necessary to drag over a hyperlinked region of text.)

2. Select **Hyperlink** from the **Properties** toolbar.

The object's properties dialog appears with the current link target shown.

- To modify the hyperlink, select a new link destination type, target, and/or options.

- To remove the hyperlink, click **No Hyperlink**.

Selecting a target window

The **Target Window** tab offers a range of target windows, frames, or a **lightbox** in which the link destination will be displayed.

To select a target window:

1. From the object's properties dialog's **Hyperlink** tab, select the **Target Window** tab.

2. Select an option from the **Type** drop-down list.

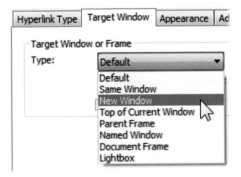

To view or edit existing hyperlinks:

- From the **Tools** menu, select **Site Manager>Hyperlink Manager** to view, rename, or remove hyperlinks.

Applying actions

Actions can be associated with objects (not text) to allow for greater user interactivity. Available actions, triggered typically by a click or mouse rollover of the object, are as follows:

- **Alert**: Displays a pop-up alert box (on click).

- **Visibility**: Displays a **panel** (on rollover/click).

- **Slide on Scroll**: Object slides horizontally from left or right, fading in when scrolled in/out of view.

- **Fade-In**: Makes objects transparent until rollover, e.g. to only show navigation buttons on panel hover over.

- **Z-Index**: Changes the order (Z-index) of the object in relation to other objects (on rollover). A high Z-index value (e.g. 150) ensures the object appears in front of other objects on rollover. For example, a usually hidden picture in a picture stack can be promoted to the front on rollover.

- **Print**: Prints the current page via a Print dialog (on click).

- **Slider**: Adds an action (Play, Pause, etc.) to a supporting navigation button to control slider playback. You can add an appropriate action to each type of navigation buttons, i.e. a Play action can be applied to a Play button. (See **Sliders** on p. 66.)

- **Slider Feedback**: Changes the button state dynamically according to the slider's current playback state.

- **Magnifier**: Areas of a picture can be hovered over for an overlaid or offset magnified view. (See p. 39.)

- **Pinterest**: Adds a clickable pin to your picture (viewable on hover over) that lets you upload your picture to a board on the picture-based social media website **Pinterest**. An account needs to be created on the Pinterest website to use this feature.

- **Custom**: Runs your own JavaScript code in response to a click, mouse, key press, and more.

> You'll need to create a panel in advance before you can assign an action to it, allowing it to display. For more information, see **Inserting panels** on p. 42.

To apply an action:

1. Select 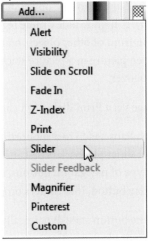 **Edit Actions** from the **Properties** toolbar.

2. From the dialog, click **Add** and choose an option from the flyout.

Add...
Alert
Visibility
Slide on Scroll
Fade In
Z-Index
Print
Slider
Slider Feedback
Magnifier
Pinterest
Custom

3. From the dialog, configure the action.

4. Click **OK**.

On previewing or publishing, a click or hover over of the object will trigger the action chosen.

Adding an anchor

An anchor is a specific location on a page that can serve as the **target** for a hyperlink (see p. 57). Invisible to the web page visitor, it typically marks a point within some text (such as the start of a particular section) or a picture at some point down the page.

To attach an anchor to a section of text:

1. Either:

    i. Use the **Pointer Tool** to click for an insertion point inside the target text.

    ii. From the **Text** menu, select **Insert>Anchor** (or press **Ctrl+Q**).
    - or -

    • Right-click anywhere inside the target text and select **Insert>Anchor**.

    The Anchor dialog opens. The anchor automatically adopts the name of the adjacent word in the target text.

2. (Optional) Rename the anchor using the **Name of the anchor** input box.

3. (Optional) Check **Include Anchor in Navigation** to allow the anchor to be accessed via a **navigation bar** instead of a hyperlink. You'll need to ensure **Include anchors** is checked on your **navigation bar settings** and that the anchor is given a title.

4. Click **OK**.

To insert an anchor to an object:

1. Use the **Pointer Tool** to select the target object.

2. Select ![icon] **ID and Anchor** from the **Properties** toolbar.

3. In the dialog, select **Treat this object as an anchor**.

4. (Optional) To assign a specific anchor identification name to your anchor (rather than using the object's HTML ID), uncheck **Use object ID** and then type a name into the **Anchor ID** input box.

5. (Optional) Check **Include Anchor in Navigation**.

6. Click **OK**.

To view or edit existing anchors:

- From the **Tools** menu, select **Site Manager>Anchor Manager** to view, rename, or remove an anchor attached to a particular object. You can also include the anchor in page navigation.

Using lightboxes

Lightboxes are a fun and modern way of displaying all kinds of web content superimposed over your web page. When you click an object, the light box presents your chosen content "on demand" in a pop-up window.

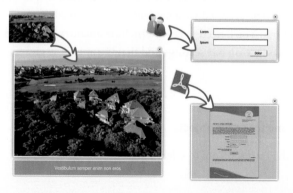

To create a lightbox for a picture on your web page:

1.   Select the picture (preferably a thumbnail).

2.   Click **Hyperlink** from the **Properties** toolbar.

3.   From the Hyperlink Type tab, select **Picture** from the menu.

4.   From the Target Window tab, choose **Lightbox** from the **Type** drop-down list.

5.   (Optional) Add a caption to the picture in the lightbox using the **Caption** box. You can also make the picture part of a slideshow using the **Slideshow Name** drop-down list.

6.   Click **OK**.

To restrict the display size of this linked "lightboxed" picture, WebPlus scales down pictures to a maximum width and height (default 800 x 600 pixels). The maximum width and height can be modified. (See **Setting site properties** on p. 22).

To create a lightbox to a local picture:

•   As above but choose the **File** option instead of Picture.

Interactive
Objects

5

Inserting sliders

Sliders are a fun and exciting way to animate **panels**, and are ideal for a whole range of uses including advertising banners, news tickers and as alternative navigation bars.

Each slider is made up of a series of panels, with just one panel visible at any one time.

Each panel can show a mixture of pictures, text, and line/shape art. Like a slideshow, each panel can be made to appear automatically at set intervals, manually via navigation buttons, or at a set time.

Various **animation styles** can be used to control how each panel is displayed.

Pre-designed professional sliders are available from the **Asset Browser**, and are typically customized once on the page using the **Slider Studio**. Panels can be added, reordered, or deleted to create the slider of your choosing.

To insert a slider:

1. From the **Quick Build tab** (Interactive Objects category), click 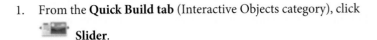 **Slider**.

2. To insert the slider where you want it to appear on the page, position the displayed cursor then simply click the mouse.

3. In the **Asset Browser** dialog, select "Sliders" in the **Pack Files** category, then select an individual slider from the main pane.

4. Click **OK**.

You can also add sliders to the page using the Assets tab (see WebPlus Help).

To select a slider:

- Select anywhere in the slider region, then click **Select Parent** in the toolbar under the selected slider.

> When added to the page, some sliders may be part of a grouped object. In this case, you can select the slider via the **Objects** tab.

Editing your slider on the page

Your slider comes with a set of placeholder panels by default. A selected slider offers navigation buttons to review each panel in the slider.

To navigate between panels:

- Click the navigation buttons directly under the selected slider.

Every slider also has a Foreground panel that displays its contents permanently. The panel is perfect for adding contact details, sale buttons, telephone numbers, or a picture that you always want to show.

One you've reviewed the content you can either edit the slider directly on the page or use the more versatile **Slider Studio**.

To edit your slider directly on the page:

1. Select your slider.

2. From the context toolbar, choose options to:

   - add, copy or delete panels.

   - name your panels.

   - apply **actions** to panels.

Using panel navigation, each panel can then be edited like a "mini-page".

Editing your slider in Slider Studio

Your slider can be fully customized to your liking within the **Slider Studio**.

The studio offers a panel-to-view display with supporting tabs for panel configuration, and lets you perform all of the operations possible from the context toolbar (above) plus additional features such as slider preview.

To edit your slider in Slider Studio:

1. Select anywhere in the slider region, then from the Slider

    context toolbar, select **Slider Studio**.

2. In the displayed Slider Studio, edit the slider using various tabs:

*   **Slider Options**: For modifying playback controls (animation styles, autoplay, panel looping and animation times).

*   **Panels**: This tab lets you **Add Panel to Slider**, **Copy Slider Panel**, **Delete Slider Panel**, **Move Left**, or **Move Right**. When adding, a blank panel is added at the end of the last panel in your slider.

*   **Panel Options**: For panel naming, background colour, panel availability (display at set times).

Inserting a Photo Gallery

In WebPlus you can add a Flash™ or JavaScript-based photo gallery to any web page, a range of eye-catching gallery types, styles, and a choice of photo navigation methods.

Gallery types

Different Flash or JavaScript gallery types can be used to create your Photo Gallery.

Professional Flash Photo Gallery
Provides a top or bottom control bar (hosting preview thumbnail rollovers) on top of your main photo display.

Professional Flash Photo Gallery (Live Feed)
As for Professional Flash Photo Gallery but photo content is sourced online from your **Flickr** photostream (as an RSS feed), another RSS 2.0-compatible image host, or SlideShowPro Director.

Flash Photo Gallery
Provides a top or bottom control bar on top of your main photo display which offers basic navigation control and/or scrollable horizontal/vertical preview thumbnail rollovers. Photo grids and photo stacks are also available. You can also accompany your photo gallery with background music.

JavaScript Photo Gallery
Like Flash Gallery but offers JavaScript-based photo galleries. Photo grids, photo stacks, and **lightboxes** are available.

Inserting a Photo Gallery

The Photo Gallery is inserted on the page, just like an individual photo, except that the currently displayed photo is surrounded by a background, navigation bar and preview thumbnails.

To insert a Photo Gallery:

1.   From the Quick Build tab (Interactive Objects Items category), click **Photo Gallery**.

2.   To insert the gallery at a default size, position the displayed cursor where you want the gallery to appear on the page, then simply click the mouse.
- or -

To set the size of the inserted gallery, drag out a region and release the mouse button.

3.   Select the **Gallery Type** as described on p. 70.

4.   Click **Next**.

To add photos to a Photo Gallery:

1.   For all Gallery types (except the Live Feed type) from the dialog, choose whether to:

•   **Add individual files**
Click the **Add Files** button to navigate to then select the

photo file(s) to open. Use **Ctrl**-click or **Shift**-click to select multiple non-adjacent or adjacent files.

- or -

Click the **Add Assets** button to navigate to then select the photo file(s) to open.

- or -

- **Add all photos in a folder**
  Click the **Add Folder** button to navigate to a folder then select it to add its content.

2. (Optional) Select any photo thumbnail(s) for manipulation;

   - To add a caption, click the **Caption** column and input text, numbers and characters.

   - (Professional Flash Photo Gallery only) To add hyperlinks to photos, click **Edit hyperlink**. From the dialog, choose a **Hyperlink Type**—you can set no hyperlink, hyperlinks to the original image, or hyperlinks to a different **link destination** (e.g., Site Page or Internet Page).

3. Click **Next**.

To select and modify a Photo Gallery style:

1. Select a Gallery style from the **Gallery Style** pane running across the top of the dialog.

2. (Optional) For the selected style, use the pane on the right to modify various gallery-wide options (autoplay, background/frame/font colour, caption and navigation bar control, etc.).

3. Click **Finish**.

Editing the Photo Gallery

Once added to the web page, the Photo Gallery can be edited at any time by double clicking.

Inserting Google Maps

Use embedded **Google Maps** in your web page if want to make sure that a client can locate your headquarters, attendees can find that special meeting (or event), or identify any other special interest locations.

Each map will allow **markers** to be placed on the map to identify locations.

To insert a Google Map:

1. Click **Google Map** from the **Quick Build** tab (Interactive Objects) and drag the insert cursor across your page to set the map size.

2.   From the Google Map dialog, enter your post code (zip code) or address in the **Search for a location** field, then click **Search**. As Google's geolocator is being used, WebPlus will sense your locale, and display local addresses preferentially.

Adding markers

You can add an unlimited number of markers to your Google Map. Each marker can display further details on hover over and mouse click.

To add a marker:

1.   From the Google Map dialog, click **Add**.

2.   In the Google Map Marker dialog, click a chosen location using the ⁻¦⁻ cursor.

3.   Enter a **Name** for the marker. This "tooltip" displays on **hover over** and could represent a company or site name.

4.   Assign a **Click action** to the marker, i.e. what gets displayed on button click.

5.   (Optional) Check **Open InfoWindow by default** for your label to display without the marker being clicked.

6.   Click **OK**. The marker appears on the map preview in green (to indicate it is currently selected). Repeat the process for each additional marker you wish to add.

Inserting rollover graphics

A picture whose appearance changes in response to a mouse event is called a **rollover graphic**. Mouse events could typically be a hover over or mouse button press.

 You can directly import rollover graphics created in Serif DrawPlus. (See WebPlus Help for more information.)

Rollover options

Creating rollovers is a matter of deciding which state(s) you'll want to define, then specifying a picture variant for each chosen state. WebPlus provides several choices:

Normal State is the "resting" state of the picture before any rollover, and is always defined.

Over State is the state triggered by a mouseover— when the mouse pointer is directly over the picture.

Down State is triggered by clicking the mouse then keeping the button depressed while on the picture.

Another state, **Down+Over** (not illustrated) implies a mouseover that occurs when the picture is already Down, i.e. after it's been clicked.

You can also specify a **hyperlink** event—for example, a jump to a targeted web page—that will trigger if the user releases the mouse button while in down state.

To create a rollover graphic:

1. In a suitable image-editing program, create the variant source pictures for each state you'll be defining.

2. Click **Rollover** from the **Quick Build** tab (Interactive Objects) and drag the insert cursor across your page to set the rollover size.

3. In the Insert Rollover dialog, on the **Rollover Graphic** tab:

   - Specify which rollover states (see above) you want to activate for each picture by checking boxes in the Rollover states section. For each one, use the **Browse** button to locate the corresponding source picture or click Browse Assets to locate pictures from your saved asset packs.

   - (Optional) Specify **Export Options** for your pictures.

   - Check **Embed files in site** if you want to incorporate the picture(s) in the site.

   - Choose either **Normal** or **Down** as the button's initial rollover state.

   - Check **Radio button** if you want to link this rollover to others on its page (that have also got this option checked), so that only one is in a 'down' state at one time.

4. Click **OK**. WebPlus displays the picture assigned to the Normal state.

To edit a rollover graphic:

- Double-click the rollover graphic, to display the Edit Rollover dialog. Modify settings as appropriate.

Inserting pop-up rollovers

The most common use for pop-up rollovers in WebPlus is to hover over a picture thumbnail to show its larger representation, usually offset next to the thumbnail.

WebPlus lets you choose the position and size of the pop-up in relation to the "hovered over" thumbnail.

To insert a pop-up rollover:

1. Click   **Pop-up Rollover** from the **Quick Build** tab (Interactive Objects) and drag the insert cursor across your page to set the rollover size.

2. From the dialog, on the **Rollover Graphic** tab:

    - For the Normal rollover image click the **Browse** button, and navigate to and select the image. Click **Open**.
      - or -
      Click the **Browse Assets** button and locate an image from your saved asset packs.

- For the Over image, the previously chosen Normal image is used by default (typically for photo thumbnails). However, you can **Browse** or **Browse Assets** to use a completely different image.

3.   Click **OK**.

If captioning is required on pop-up rollovers this can be made to appear next to your Over image (see WebPlus Help for details).

For pop-up rollovers to work effectively you'll need to position the Normal and Over images on your page. Positioning is carried out from a dedicated dialog, where each state image can be moved and resized by dragging (or by setting absolute pixel values). See WebPlus Help for more information.

To edit a pop-up rollover:

- Double-click the Normal image on the page, to display the Edit Pop-Up Rollover dialog. Modify settings as appropriate.

Smart Objects

6

Login forms

WebPlus lets you add a login/logout form onto a page in your website. This means that a registered web visitor can gain access to any restricted pages by signing in to the site.

The login box is part of your Site Membership Manager in Serif Web Resources. Registered users can either be added manually via **www.serifwebresources.com** or via self-registration user sign up.

To insert a login form:

1. From the **Quick Build** tab (Smart Objects category), click **Login Form**.

2. Position the cursor where you want the form to be placed, then click the mouse.

3. If you don't have a Serif Web Resources account (or are logged out), you'll get the Serif Web Resources login dialog. To sign up, click **Create Account** under the **New User?** section.
    - or -
    If you're an existing user and are already logged in, you'll get a Site Membership Managers dialog.

4. From the Site Membership Managers dialog, select the Site Membership Manager for your site. If you haven't already

created one, click **Create New**. (See **Site Membership Manager** on p. 99)

5.   In the Edit dialog, several options are available:

*   Click **Configure** to set the appearance of your form.

*   Click **Manage** to access **www.serifwebresources.com** to set up your Site Membership Manager.

*   From the Appearance settings box, set a colour for your background, border, text/labels, and buttons.

6.   Click **Insert** to add the form to your page.

Inserting a blog

A blog acts as a personal journal on your web page that hosts your own published articles and offers an easy-to-use text editor. Articles can be commented on by visitors to the web page.

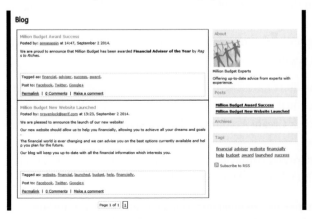

In WebPlus, blogs are actually **Smart Objects**, a common term to indicate that they are intelligent server-sided objects hosted on the secure online service called **Serif Web Resources**. As a result, a prerequisite to using blogs, like all Smart Objects, is that you create a valid Serif Web Resources account and a Site Membership Manager for your site in advance.

As a blog owner, you can manage the blog. Articles can be added, edited, or removed, while visitor's article comments can be deleted. Another feature is the ability to allow multiple authors to add articles to your blog (see WebPlus Help).

 If you're on the move or working remotely, you can always monitor and update this managed content by using **Serif Web Resources**. A republish of your website is not necessary.

Inserting blogs

Blogs are like any object in WebPlus, in that you can easily insert one onto a chosen page.

To insert a blog (on the page):

1. From the **Quick Build** tab (Smart Objects), click **Blog**.

2. Drag the cursor across your page to define the size of your blog region.

3. If you don't have a Serif Web Resources account (or are logged out), you'll get the Serif Web Resources login dialog. To sign up, click **Create Account** under the **New User?** section.
    - or -
    If you're an existing user and are already logged in, you'll get a Site Membership Managers dialog.

4. From the Site Membership Managers dialog, select the Site Membership Manager for your site. If you haven't already created one, click **Create New**. (See **Site Membership Manager** on p. 99)

5. From the Configure dialog, enter a **Name** for your blog. This is the blog title that appears at the top of the published blog.

6. Click **Save**.

> If you've created a Site Membership Manager previously, steps 3 and 4 are not required.

> Once added to the page, you can **Edit**, **Configure**, and **Manage** the blog by right-clicking the box (or using the context toolbar).

Your blog can be edited to change its appearance and number of articles to view.

To edit your blog:

*   Double-click the blog.

> For more details about Serif Web Resources account control, see **Using Smart Objects** (p. 92).

Managing your blog

Managing your blog lets you add, edit, or delete articles, and edit comments associated with articles. You can also select an **Editor group** for multi-author article publishing. For new articles (or when editing) you can create/edit your article in RTF, add tags, pick an article poster, allow trackbacks, and make comments.

To manage your blog:

*   Select the blog and click **Manage** from the context toolbar.

> For more management information and a description of each option, click the Help button in the blog's Smart Object dialog.

For more information about Smart Objects, see WebPlus Help.

Inserting a forum

WebPlus lets you insert a **forum** Smart Object into your site, which can be structured into separate categories containing one or more subforums.

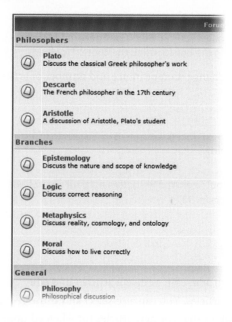

For example, you could create the categories Philosophers, Branches, and General, while the Philosophers category would include the subforums Plato, Descarte, and Aristotle.

Visitors can view the topics posted in a subforum, the number of replies/views, the topic author, and the last post.

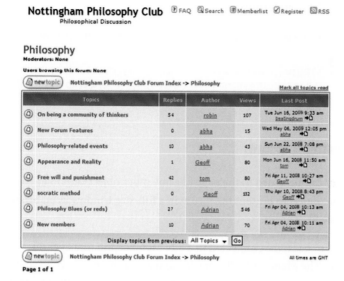

Within a selected subforum, a topic can be created by a forum visitor which can be viewed and/or optionally replied to by other forum visitors (by posting a message in response). This discussion forms the basis of forum debate, creating a "thread" of visitor replies.

Forum contributors simply register and enter their own login details to post or reply to topics.

Forum features

- Create different **categories** (e.g., Philosophers) containing multiple **subforums** (Plato, Aristotle, Descartes, etc.).

- Establish **access control** for users and moderators.

- Set forum **privacy** as publicly readable or private.

- Apply a **theme** (style) to the whole forum.

- Create, edit, and assign **user ranks**.

- Set **user permissions**.

- **Manage** and **moderate** the forum without republishing.

> If you're on the move or working remotely, you can always monitor and update this managed content by using **Serif Web Resources**. A republish of your website is not necessary.

Inserting a forum

A forum can be added to the page like any other object, although you have the option to present the forum in a full-size window as an **offsite link** instead.

The forum has to be connected to a Site Membership Manager on creation. The Manager is site-specific and acts as both a "hub" to store Smart Objects such as forums and provides user access control to your forum. You manage your Site Membership Manager in **Serif Web Resources**.

To insert a forum (on a page):

1. From the **Quick Build** tab (Smart Objects category), click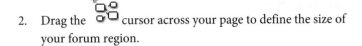
   Forum.

2. Drag the 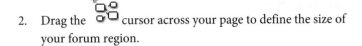 cursor across your page to define the size of your forum region.

3. If you don't have a Serif Web Resources account (or are logged out), you'll get the Serif Web Resources login dialog. To sign up, click **Create Account** under the **New User?** section.
   - or -
   If you're an existing user and are already logged in, you'll get a Site Membership Managers dialog.

4. From the Site Membership Managers dialog, select the Site Membership Manager for your site. If you haven't already created one, click **Create New**. (See **Site Membership Manager** on p. 99.)

5. From the Configure dialog, enter a **Name** for your forum. This is the forum title that appears at the top of the published forum.

6. Add a **Forum Description** to describe what the forum is for.

7. Click **Save**. The forum appears on your page.

> Once added to the page, you can Edit, Configure, and Manage the forum by right-clicking the box (or using the context toolbar).

> You can also create a forum by selecting Smart Object from the Insert menu.

To edit your forum:

• Double-click the forum.

> For more details about Serif Web Resources account control, see **Using Smart Objects** (p. 92).

Managing your forum

Up to now, you've just created a default forum—a single subforum within a single category. To edit category name, subforum name, and add more categories and/or subforums within those categories, your **Site Membership Manager** in **Serif Web Resources** has to be used. The Manager also lets you set up forum security such as creating moderators, adding users manually, banning or suspending users, along with controlling forum privacy, applying themes, and controlling user ranking (most posts).

To manage your forum:

- Select the forum and click 🔲 **Manage** from the context toolbar.

Forums, by their nature, are complex objects. For more configuration details and a description of options, click the Help button in any Smart Object dialog.

Inserting a site search

WebPlus offers a choice of powerful search options depending on how (and what part of) your website is to be searched. The two search options available are:

- **Online Search**: A user's search terms match with text content on pages in your site, including those containing text frames, tables, and Smart Objects such as blogs, forums, CMS, etc. Smart tags can be assigned to pages in advance to limit searching to just those pages.

- **Client-side Search** (as in WebPlus X7): A user's search terms match with text that appears throughout your entire site in text frames or tables only. Use for basic sites if you're not using Smart Objects or you don't need selective page searching.

🔲 The Online Search option uses **Serif Web Resources** to perform the search so you'll need to have a Serif Web Resources account and a Site Membership Manager created in the account to use the feature.

🔲 Neither search option can search offsite links, only pages in your site.

For both options, the search facility is created by combining a **Site Search Form** object with a **Site Search Results Frame**.

Site Search Results Frame—
creates a frame in which the
search results are displayed.
Typically, this is placed and sized
onto its own page, and does not
appear in the site navigation
structure.

You'll normally position the
search results frame ahead of
adding the **Site Search Form**.

Site Search Form object—the text
box in which users type the word
or phrase they want to search for.
This object is usually added to a
master page so it appears on all
pages of the site.

The search results show a hyperlinked page name heading plus
associated web page text for reference. Visitors simply click the
hyperlink to access the web page.

Setting up Online Search

Online Search uses **Serif Web Resources** to allow searching of page text
content including server-sided blog, forum, and CMS content. For
searching, a Site Membership Manager will need to be created for your
website. You may have already created one as you've created Smart
Objects but if not, you'll be asked to create a Serif Web Resources
account and then a Site Membership Manager if you don't already have
one. (See **Creating a Site Membership Manager** on p. 95.)

To add Site Search Results:

1. Choose **Site Search** from the **Insert** menu and select **Site Search Results** from the submenu (placing your search results window on your page *after* configuring it).

    - or -

2. Select **Site Search Results Frame** on the **Quick Build** tab (Smart Objects) and drag the insert cursor across your page to place your search results window.

3. From the dialog, select various options to alter the appearance of results text and/or hyperlink text.

    Keep the search results on a separate page which can have its own look and feel (double-click the object to alter site results appearance).

To add a Site Search Form:

1. (Optional) Select a master page from the Pages tab to allow the search form to be displayed across the site.

2. Choose **Site Search** from the **Insert** menu and select **Site Search Form** from the submenu. Click the insert cursor to place your site search form object.

    - or -

    Drag **Site Search Form** from the **Quick Build** tab (Smart Objects) onto your page.

3. From the Insert Site Search Form dialog, enable the **Online Search**.

4. Select the previously created search results object from the **Results Object** drop-down list.

5. To set up Smart Search Properties via **Serif Web Resources**, click **Select Site Membership Manager**. In the dialog, select the Site Manager for your site from the list or click **Create New** to create a new Site Manager.

> The Site Membership Manager must be using the same URL as your website. If they do not match the Online Search feature won'tt work.

6. (Optional) Check **Use custom text..** to display a message while search results are being compiled ready to display.

7. Check a tag name from the Smart Search Tags box to restrict searching to just the pages previously assigned that tag via **Page Properties**.

8. (Optional) Use the other tabs to control the appearance and properties of the search form.

To edit the appearance of site search form or site search results frame:

• Double-click the search object, to display its edit dialog. Modify settings as appropriate.

Adding Smart search tags to pages

The Online Search option can be made to search only pages that have been previously tagged with a Smart tag. When configuring your Site Search Form you can then select the tag names to restrict your search.

To add a Smart tag:

1. Right-click a page, and select **Page Properties**.

2. From the **Search Engine>Smart Search Tags** menu option, type your tag in the **New tag** field.

3. Click ⊕ **Add**.

Indexing your website

Once you've published your site, an important final step is to initiate the indexing of the site. This will allow web visitors to use the Online Search feature without delay.

To index your website:

- Go to your website's page containing your search form, then carry out a search for any search term present in your site.

To monitor the indexing status of your site at any time, go to your Site Membership Manager on **www.serifwebresources.com** and select the **Advanced** tab, then the **Site Search** tab.

If you make major changes to your site content subsequently you can manually force a re-index at any time by accessing the Site Search tab, and clicking **Force Reindex**. You are only limited to a few re-indexes per month.

 Site Search may be unavailable for a time while page content is indexed.

Using Smart Objects

For managed content, WebPlus uses server-sided **Smart Objects** which store gathered web visitor data on Serif's own secure server space called **Serif Web Resources**. You can manage your smart objects directly from within WebPlus, or independently, and at any time, via **www.serifwebresources.com**.

Let's look at each Smart Object you'll find in Serif Web Resources and what you can do with them.

 **Accommodation Booker**

Host the online booking of guest house, motel, and bed & breakfast rooms, with pricing options for different date periods and days of the week.

 Blog

A blog acts as a personal journal on your web page which hosts your own published articles in an easy-to-use text editing window. Articles can be commented on by visitors to the web page.

> You can also drag a blog onto the page via the Quick Build tab.

 **Content Management System (CMS)**

Lets the web developer add content to web pages remotely without accessing and publishing via WebPlus. Content is article-based where articles can be created, edited, deleted and arranged into categories. Site visitors can comment on and rate any article.

 Forum

Add a thread-based discussion forum to your site, split into multiple categories and subforums.

> You can also drag a forum onto the page via the Quick Build tab.

 News

Add a news window onto your page.

> You can also drag a news window onto the page via the Quick Build tab.

Poll

Set up an online poll to canvass web visitors' opinions.

 Resource Booker

Host the online booking of meeting rooms, rehearsal rooms, theatre tickets, and more. Book by the hour or by the day, as recurring bookings, and with pricing options for different age groups.

 Shout Box

Acts as an interactive chat window. Let your web visitors chat amongst themselves.

 As Smart Objects are stored in Serif Web Resources, you can use Help buttons accompanying each Smart Object (as you create and manage them) for more detailed information.

For security reasons, the objects are only available via a **Serif Web Resources** login accessible from within WebPlus. If you don't have a valid username and password you must create a Serif Web Resources account first.

To create a Serif Web Resources account:

1. From the **Insert** menu, select **Smart Object**.

2. In the login dialog, complete the **New User?** form. You'll need to review and agree to Serif's terms and conditions of use (via a check box).

3. Click the **Signup** button.

4. An additional dialog, will ask for personal details, plus a few check boxes if you would like to receive the Serif Community newsletter, Serif offers, and/or other third-party offers.

5. A confirmation email will be sent to your email address. Click the link in the email and you're ready to login to Serif Web Resources (via **Insert>Smart Object** or **www.serifwebresources.com**).

To clear Account details:

- Go to **Tools>Options** and click **Clear Account Details** shown from the **Options>General** menu option. This will clear the stored login details for Serif Web Resources so that automatic login will no longer work. Details will need to be entered next time so be sure you've remembered your password.

To access Serif Web Resources:

1. From the **Insert** menu, select **Smart Object**.

2. At the login prompt enter your username and your password. Check **Remember account details** to access Web Resources directly in future (bypassing the login screen).

3. Click the **Login** button.

To log out of Serif Web Resources:

- From the Smart Objects dialog, click the cog icon and select **Log out**.

Creating a Site Membership Manager

If you're a new user you have to create a **Site Membership Manager** for your site to allow Smart Objects to be created. Think of the Manager as a "hub" for the Smart Objects you want to include in your site.

> The Site Membership Manager is also used to control access to some Smart Objects such as forums and blogs, as well as providing access control to pages. See **Setting up your Site Membership Manager** on p. 100.

Once your Site Membership Manager is created, Smart Objects can be created from it, configured, and edited before adding to the web page immediately or at a later date.

Creating Smart Objects

A Smart Object can be created from a selected Site Membership Manager. Typically you would only add a single forum to your site, but your site could have multiple blogs, news objects, shout boxes, and polls spread throughout your site. Each object needs to be created in the Site Membership Manager.

Before going any further, bear in mind that the same Smart Object can be inserted into your site multiple times, optionally changing its appearance and how it displays. (See **Editing Smart Objects** on p. 97.)

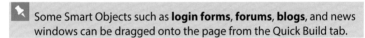

Some Smart Objects such as **login forms**, **forums**, **blogs**, and news windows can be dragged onto the page from the Quick Build tab.

To create a Smart Object:

1. From the **Insert** menu, select **Smart Object**.

2. From the Site Membership Managers dialog, select the manager entry for the site you want to add a Smart Object to.

3. From the Insert Smart Objects dialog, click **New**.

4. In the Create Smart Object dialog, use the scroll bar to navigate the list, then select a Smart Object.

5. Click **OK**.

Configuring Smart Objects

The created Smart Object needs to be named, given a description, and, in some cases, have settings configured to control the way the Smart Object operates.

1. From the Configure dialog:

    *   Enter your own **Name** for the object. This displays next to the Smart Object under the Site Membership Manager entry for easy identification.

    *   Set the **Language** to be used for your object.

    *   Depending on the Smart Object type, settings will vary. Use the **Help** button on each Smart Object's Configure dialog for a detailed description of each option.

2. Click **Create**.

Once on your page, you can re-configure the Smart Object by right-clicking and selecting **Configure**.

Editing Smart Objects

Editing the Smart Object means changing the appearance of the object to suit your site's design. Typically, you might want to alter the appearance of the object from its original settings. The settings depend on the type of object selected.

Once an object is created it can be edited either from your Site Membership Manager or directly on the page.

To edit a Smart Object from your Site Membership Manager:

*   From the Edit dialog's Appearance Settings, select a background colour and configure other settings depending on the type of Smart Object.

Selecting an object from within the Smart Objects library view (having expanded the Site Membership Manager) will also open the Edit dialog.

To edit a Smart Object on your page:

- Double-click the object to reveal the object's Edit dialog.

> Editing an object only affects the object on the page and does not alter any collected data.

> You can insert multiple instances of the same Smart Object. Each separate instance can then be edited independently.

Adding Smart Objects to your page

To add a Smart Object to your web page:

1. From the Edit dialog, click the **Insert** button.

2. To insert the object at a default size, position the ✛ 🏁 cursor where you want the object to appear on the page, then simply click the mouse.

   - or -

   Drag the cursor across the page to size the Smart Object.

The Smart Object will automatically preview on the page so you'll get a good feel for how your published Smart Object will look.

Managing Smart Objects

While configuring Smart Objects affects how the object operates, managing Smart Objects can be used to manage the object's "gathered" data when the web page is published. More complex Smart Objects (e.g., a Forum, Blog, Accommodation Booker, Resource Booker, Poll, or

Shout Box) store collected visitor data such as article comments, email addresses, poll results, and a chat messaging log. For example, for **Blogs** creating and managing articles is a fundamental part of the management process.

To manage a Smart Object from your Site Membership Manager:

1. From your Site Membership Manager, double-click the Smart Object.

2. From the Edit dialog, click **Manage**. The management options differ for each Smart Object type.

    You'll be taken to Serif Web Resources where you can manage your Smart Object.

> Once on your page, you can manage the Smart Object by right-clicking and selecting **Manage**.

> For more management information and a description of each option, click the Help button in any Smart Object dialog.

> If you're on the move or working remotely, you can always monitor and update this managed content by using **Serif Web Resources**. A republish of your website is not necessary.

Site Membership Manager

The Site Membership Manager in **Serif Web Resources** serves two functions:

*   You can apply security to your site, either to restrict access to specific pages or to control which users can access **forums**, edit **blog** articles or create CMS content.

*   The Site Membership Manager acts as a "hub" for creating, editing and managing **Smart Objects** such as blogs and forums.

Only one Site Membership Manager can be created per website. If you're a multi-site developer you'll be able to manage multiple websites via each site's Site Membership Manager. Each Site Membership Manager controls its own unique access control arrangements and Smart Objects.

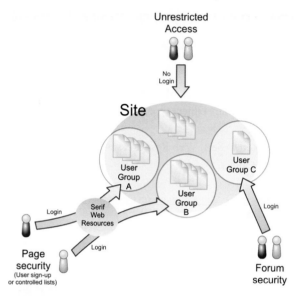

See WebPlus Help for more information.

> If you want to create Smart Objects, see **Using Smart Objects** on p. 92.

Setting up your Site Membership Manager

> The Site Membership Manager is also used to manage Smart Objects such as blogs and forums in your site.

To create a Site Membership Manager:

1. From the **Insert** menu, select **Smart Object**.

2. Log in to Serif Web Resources (See **Using Smart Objects** on p. 92). This assumes you have a valid login; otherwise you will have to **register**.

3. From the Site Membership Managers dialog, select **Create New**.

4. In the Configure dialog, you have to set up a **Site Name**. This is a server-side manager that needs to be created to allow Smart Object and access control to operate.

5. Enter the **Site URL**, which is the web address of your site, e.g. www.rainbow.org.uk.

6. Click **Create**. The Site Membership Manager is added as an entry.

7. Click the entry to offer various access control options you might like in your site.

Display options

The Site Membership Manager provides several different display options which can be added to your page.

Member Login Form: Use this option to add a login form directly to your page. Typically of use in personal websites or small enterprise websites, you can allow free access to most of your site, with only a limited set of pages accessible to selected web visitors via login.

 This login form can also be added via the Quick Build tab.

See **Login forms** on p. 80 for more information.

Mailing List Signup: Have website visitors sign up to newsletters, party confirmations, information request, and many more. Lists can be controlled manually or by self-subscription. Email addresses can be imported as a delimited text file (CSV) or exported to a range of formats.

See **Mailing lists** on p. 104 for more information.

Protecting pages with passwords

For some pages you may want to restrict access to only a selected group of users.

WebPlus uses Serif Web Resources to control which users can access the page. Login details are stored in a user group associated with the page which contains a list of authorized users.

To set up your user access control:

1. Create a new Site Membership Manager for your site. (See **Site Membership Manager** on p. 99.)

2. Login to **www.serifwebresources.com**.

3. From the Groups tab, enter a group name and click **Create Group**.

4. From the Members tab, enter a member's email address in the **Email** field, and click **Add Member**.

5. Check members to be added from the list, click the **Select Action** drop-down list, then select **Add to Group**.

6. Check the group name, then click **OK**.

To protect your page with a password:

1. Right-click the page in the Pages tab, and choose **Page Properties**, then select **Page Security**.

2. Check **Protect page with password** to enable access control. You'll notice that the **Change/Manage** button becomes active. Click this button to reveal currently available user groups (in bold) and the Site Membership Manager to which they belong.

3.   From the User Groups dialog, select the user group, e.g. Members (which belongs to the website Rainbow), then click **OK**. Your page's Page Security tab should show that the page is password protected and that the user group has been assigned.

4.   Click **OK**, then **OK** again to exit the dialogs.

Mailing lists

As well as **login forms**, mailing lists can be created in WebPlus. A mailing list can be added onto a page in your website which allows web visitors to sign up to newsletters, etc.

The mailing list box is part of your **Site Membership Manager**.

To create a mailing list:

1.   Select **Insert>Smart Object**.

2.   From the dialog, select the Site Membership Manager for your site. If you haven't already created one, click **Create New**.

3.   From the dialog, select **Mailing List Signup**.

4.   In the Edit dialog, several options are available:

   •   Click **Configure** to set the appearance of your mailing list.

   •   Click **Manage** to access **www.serifwebresources.com** to manage your mailing lists.

   •   From the Appearance settings box, set a colour for your background, border, text/labels, and buttons.

5.   Click **Insert** to add the mailing list box to your page.

Social Media

7

Inserting a Facebook widget

Facebook widgets can be added to your page to stream various types of live feeds to display on your page or a Like button that allows users to share and promote your page via their Facebook pages.

 A Facebook account is recommended to use these widgets. For more information about Facebook, visit **www.facebook.com**.

Inserting a Facebook widget

The widget is placed directly on the page, the same as any other object.

To insert a Facebook widget:

1. From the Quick Build tab (Social Media category), click  **Facebook Widget** then click on the page to place.

2. In the dialog, from the **Type** drop-down list, select either **Activity Feed**, **Like Feed**, **Recommendations Feed**, or **Like Button**.

3. In the Preview pane, check or uncheck **Update** to preview what your widget will look like on the page as you make changes.

4.   Customize the behaviour of your widget:

- **Use Current Site URL**
  Check to use the current URL of your site. Uncheck to
  enter a custom web address below. For Like Feed, enter the
  exact URL of a Facebook page.

- **Link Target** (Recommendations Feed only)
  Select **Blank** to open links in a new window, select **Parent**
  or **Top** to open links in the same window.

- **Verb to Display** (Like Button only)
  Select **Like** or **Recommend** as the word that appears on the
  button.

5.   (Optional) Customize the appearance of your widget using
     additional options (these differ according to Type).

6.   Click **OK**.

Editing a Facebook widget

Once added to the page, the Facebook widget can be edited at any time.

To edit a Facebook widget:

1.   Double-click the widget. The Edit dialog is displayed. The
     options available are the same as those available when the
     widget was created.

2.   Make your changes and click **OK**.

You can add an anchor to your widget by clicking Anchor on the
context toolbar. For more information on anchors, see **Adding an
anchor** on p. 61.

Inserting a Twitter widget

A Tweet or Follow button can be added to your page that interfaces directly with Twitter.

 A Twitter account is recommended to use these widgets. For more information about Twitter, visit **www.twitter.com**.

Twitter widget types

There are two types of widgets that can be added to a page to allow visitors to engage with site content in different ways.

Tweet Button   Allows visitors to share your website by tweeting your site content to their Twitter profile.

Follow Button   Allows visitors to follow your account on Twitter.

Inserting a Twitter widget

The widget is placed directly onto the page, the same as any other object.

To insert a Tweet Button:

1.   From the Quick Build tab (Social Media category), click **Twitter Widget** then click on the page to place.

2. In the dialog, from the **Type** drop-down list, select **Tweet Button**.

3. Customize the behaviour of your button:

    - **Use Current Site URL**
      Check to use the current URL of your site. Uncheck to enter a custom web address in **URL To Tweet**.

    - **Tweet Text**
      Enter Tweet Text. This text gets displayed in the Tweet field and is modifiable prior to Tweet submission.

    - **Via**
      Enter the name of a Twitter account to add to the end of the tweet as a "via @<username>". It is recommended to enter your username in this field.

    - **Recommend**
      Offers a recommended Twitter username that web visitors can follow. The recommendation appears after a Tweet has been submitted.

    - **Hashtag**
      Enter a phrase as a hashtag (phrases cannot have spaces). Tweets will be searchable by that hashtag.

4. (Optional) Customize the appearance of your widget using additional options (these differ according to Type).

5. Click **OK**.

To insert a Follow Button:

1. From the Quick Build tab (Social Media category), click **Twitter Widget** then click on the page to place.

2. In the dialog, from the **Type** drop-down list, select **Follow Button**.

3. In the Preview pane, check or uncheck **Update** to preview what your widget will look like on the page as you make changes.

4. In **User To Follow**, enter a Twitter username. Visitors will follow this account on Twitter when they click your button.

5. (Optional) Customize the appearance of your widget using additional options (these differ according to Type).

6. Click **OK**.

Editing a Twitter widget

Once added to the page, the Twitter widget can be edited at any time.

To edit a Twitter widget:

- Double-click the widget.

Inserting a Google +1 button

Promote your site by using a Google +1 button to let visitors recommend your site content to **Google+**. When visitors click your button they will be able to share your web page by posting on their live stream or the +1 tab on their Google+ profiles. The +1 tab displays all links a user recommends to the public. The Google +1 button can also display how many others have recommended your web page.

 A Google+ account is recommended to use this button. To find out more about Google+, visit **plus.google.com**.

To insert a Google +1 button:

1. From the Quick Build tab (Social Media category), click
   Google +1 Button then click on the page.

2. From the dialog, in the Preview pane, check or uncheck **Update** to preview what your widget will look like on the page as you make changes.

3. In the Configuration pane, check **+1 Current Page** to use the current URL of your site. Uncheck to enter a custom web address in **Custom URL**.

4. (Optional) From the **Size** drop-down list, select a size for your widget.

5. (Optional) From the **Annotation** drop-down list, select an annotation style.

6. Click **OK**.

To edit a Google +1 button:

• Double-click the button.

Inserting a social bookmarking button strip

If you add a strip containing a selection of social bookmarking buttons, your web visitors can share and promote your site via whichever social media or social news site is clicked. WebPlus lets you to create a strip with some of the most popular social websites including Facebook, Twitter, Reddit, Digg, etc.

Although not considered social media, the strip also lets visitors share your site's URL via email or simply print the current page.

> Why not position your button strip on a master page? This will make the strip available across all pages that use that master page.

To insert a social bookmarking button strip:

1. From the Quick Build tab (Social Media category), click **Social Bookmarking Button Strip** then click anywhere on the page to place it.

2. From the dialog, select a website from the **Not Included In Strip** list and click **Add** to add that website's button to the strip. To remove a button from the strip, select a website from the **Included In Strip** list and click **Remove**.

3. (Optional) Click **Up** or **Down** to change the order icons appear on your strip.

4. Select a **Share** option: **Site** to share your entire site, or **Page** to share just the page.

5. Click **OK**.

To edit a social bookmarking button strip:

- Double-click the button strip.

Media

8

Inserting videos

WebPlus includes an optimized and highly-compatible video player from Flowplayer that lets you place individual videos and playlists directly on your page. You can use locally stored videos, uploaded videos on your web space or stream videos that exist elsewhere online. The player is versatile with a customizable appearance that gives viewers access to all the playback controls they'd expect, including watching videos full-screen.

Supported video formats

The primary supported video format is MP4 (.mp4). For extended compatibility, Flowplayer can supplement MP4 video with WebM (.webm) and Ogg Video (.ogv) variants to use where MP4 is not supported. Flowplayer achieves excellent compatibility using the modern HTML5 standard to stream video without requiring a browser plug-in. On older browsers, where HTML5 is not supported, Flowplayer can fallback to using a Flash Player instead.

To insert a single video or playlist:

1. From the Quick Build tab (Media category), click **Video Player**.

2. Position the cursor where you want the video player to appear on the page, then simply click the mouse.

3. Choose the format for your video player:

   - **Use HTML5 and MP4 video**
     HTML5 offers the **best compatibility** playback with no browser plug-in or media playing software required.
     - or -

- **Use Flash video**
  Choose the older Flash video player for Flash FLV video.

4. Add your video or videos to the player:

  - **Add individual videos**
    Click the **Add Files** button to select the video file(s) to open.
    - or -

  - **Add all videos in a folder**
    Click the **Add Folder** button then navigate to a folder, select it and click **OK** to add its content.
    - or -

  - **Add videos from your Assets**
    Click the **Add Assets** button then choose your preferred player format and click **OK.**
    - or -

  - **Add a video previously uploaded using Online Resource Manager**
    Click **Add URL** and enable **Add from Online Resources**. From the drop-down list, select the file.
    - or -

  - **Add a video that is already online**
    Click **Add URL** and paste or type an online video URL (its full web address). This could be a video on another website.

5. (Optional) To remove a video from the playlist, check the box to the left of its thumbnail and click **Delete**.

6. (Optional) To adjust video order in a playlist, use the ⏶ **Up** and ⏷ **Down** buttons at the bottom of the dialog.

7. Click **OK**.

See **Inserting Videos** in WebPlus Help for further information about player and playlist configuration.

The video player will be inserted where you clicked on your page and by default will be sized to match the first video in your playlist. You can **configure the player** to adjust its size and appearance and also customize playlist control buttons.

 Online Resource Manager (**Tools>Site Manager**) can be used to scan your web space for video files, as well as manually upload videos to your web space. Any video file showing in the **Online Resource Manager** will be available from the above **Add from Online Resources** drop-down list.

To replace a video or edit the playlist

For an existing video player, you can go back to your video selection or playlist and edit it at any time.

To replace your video or edit the playlist:

1. Double-click the video object on your page.

2. Follow **Steps 4 to 7 above** to add videos, delete a video, reorder the playlist, or add WebM and Ogg videos to supplement MP4 files.

Resize and configure the video player

Customize the size and basic appearance of the video player while setting it up or at any time afterwards.

To customize a video player:

1. Double-click an existing video on your page and click the **Settings** tab.

2. Choose a clip or predefined dimensions from the **Size** list on the **General** tab to set the player size. It's recommended that your player is sized to match your video (or smaller) rather than choosing a player size larger than your clips.

3. Choose a **Skin** to set the player's basic appearance.

4. Pick **Colours** for your progress bar and other elements.

5. Replace the **Poster image**—the preview shown in the player before your video or playlist begins.

6. Choose the **Controls** that you would like viewers to be able to use.

7. Set optional player **Behaviour**.

8. Enable or disable player **Controls**, such as the mute button, volume slider, and 'get embed code' button for sharing videos on other sites.

9. (Optional) Click **Assets** to save these configuration settings to your Assets for future use, where they can simply be dragged and dropped onto a video object from the Asset tab to load your preferred settings.

You can customize the player even further if you have multiple videos in a playlist by choosing new **Playlist Buttons**.

Adding and customizing playlist control buttons

When you have more than one video in a playlist viewers can use buttons to select another video from the sequence, or skip to the previous/next video in the list. You can also customize these buttons using ready-made artwork and buttons of your own design.

Inserting YouTube videos

YouTube videos that are already published on the Internet can be included on your web page. YouTube videos themselves are not embedded in your site; instead, just the unique video ID is embedded as you place the YouTube video on your page.

To embed a single YouTube video:

1. Open the www.youtube.com website in your browser, and choose the YouTube video that you want to link to.

2. Copy the URL address for the video (or embed code). This contains an alphanumeric ID which uniquely identifies the video clip.

3. From the Quick Build tab (Media category), select **You Tube** **YouTube** and click on your page.

4. In the dialog, ensure that Single Video is listed in the **Choose a video selection** drop down. Paste the video URL, ID, or embed code into the input box.

5.   (Optional) To just play a snippet rather than the full video, specify start and end times (in seconds).

6.   Click **OK** if you are happy to insert the video in a standard YouTube player.

To swap your YouTube video for another, double-click an existing YouTube video. From the dialog, paste a previously copied video URL into the input box. Consider embedding a **YouTube playlist** instead of a fixed choice of individual videos if you want to update video content on your site without using WebPlus.

Inserting Vimeo videos

Vimeo videos that are already published on the Internet can be included on your web page. Videos themselves are not embedded in your site; instead, just the unique Vimeo video ID is embedded as you place the Vimeo video on your page.

To embed a Vimeo video:

1.   Open the www.vimeo.com website in your browser, and choose the Vimeo video that you want to link to.

2. Copy the URL address for the video (or its embed code). This contains an alphanumeric ID which uniquely identifies the video clip.

3. From the Quick Build tab (Media category), select **Vimeo** and click on your page.

4. In the dialog, paste the video URL into the input box.

5. (Optional) Choose a custom colour for the player controls and any visible text to match or contrast with your site using the **Colour of Video Controls** selector.

6. (Optional) Check/Uncheck the boxes to enable/disable

7. Click **OK**.

Inserting audio

WebPlus includes an audio player from jPlayer that uses HTML 5 for wide compatibility. On your page using the player, you can include a single audio file, or add multiple tracks to make your own playlist. You can use audio from your own computer, or stream audio that exists elsewhere online. The "skin" of your player can be customized to give it a different theme if you want to. Playback controls such as play, stop, next and previous are provided.

Supported audio format

The primary supported audio format is MP3 (.mp3). However, where MP3 is not supported, the audio player can supplement MP3 audio by using alternative delivery formats as a fallback.

Adding audio to your page

Audio is inserted in a player straight onto the page. You can add audio from a file, from assets, or from an already online or uploaded location.

To insert a single audio or a playlist:

1. From the Quick Build tab (Media category), click **Audio Player**.

2. Position the cursor where you want the audio player to appear on the page, then simply click the mouse.

3. In the **Insert Audio Player** dialog on the **Audio Player** tab, add your audio:

   - **Add individual audio**
     Click the **Add Files** button to select the file(s) to open.
     - or -

   - **Add all audio files in a folder**
     Click the **Add Folder** button then navigate to a folder, select it and click **OK** to add its content.
     - or -

   - **Add audio from your Assets**
     Click the **Add Assets** button then choose your preferred player format and click **OK.**
     - or -

   - **Add audio previously uploaded via Online Resource Manager**
     Click **Add URL** and enable **Add from Online Resources**. From the drop-down list, select the file.
     - or -

- **Add audio that is already online**
  Click **Add URL** and paste or type an online audio URL (its full web address). This could be audio on another website.

4. (Optional) To remove audio from the playlist, check the box to the left of its thumbnail and click **Delete**.

5. (Optional) To adjust order in a playlist, use the ⏶ **Up** and ⏷ **Down** buttons at the bottom of the dialog.

6. Click **OK**.

The audio player will be inserted where you clicked on your page.

> **Online Resource Manager** (**Tools>Site Manager**) can be used to scan your web space for audio files, as well as manually upload audio to your web space. Any audio file showing in the **Online Resource Manager** will be available from the above **Add from Online Resources** drop-down list.

To change the audio player theme

You can choose a different theme which changes the appearance of your audio player. If you have multiple audio players, they must share the same theme.

1. Select **Properties menu>Site Properties>Features>Audio Player**.

2. In the **Select Theme** drop-down list, choose a theme.

3. Click **OK**.

Forms

9

Inserting forms

Web-based forms allow information to be collected from visitors to your website in an efficient and modern manner.

Form data can be collected in a variety of ways—by email, to a local/remote script file, or via Serif Web Resources. See **Submission of forms** on p. 131.

Form Structure

The building blocks of a form comprise a mixture of text labels and form fields. A field can be for a button, edit box, date picker, text area, combo box, check box, radio button, file upload, or CAPTCHA object. A typical form, perhaps an email feedback form, is made up of a combination of some of these fields.

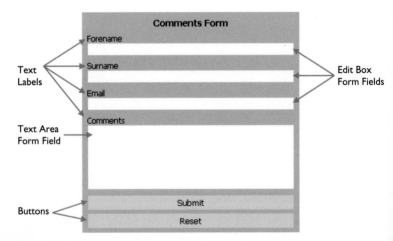

From the web visitor's perspective, information is typed into text boxes or selected from check boxes, radio buttons, or drop-down boxes. The information entered can be numeric, textual, or a mixture of both, depending on the type of field. The tab order by which fields are to be completed is configurable, as is validation of input data. (See WebPlus Help for more about tab order and validation).

Each field has its own set of properties relating to its appearance, its value(s), validation, or the action expected of the field.

A form's functionality only becomes active when your website is published (of course you can still preview your forms from within WebPlus, see **Previewing your site** on p. 155). When a web visitor enters data into, or selects a form option, the data will be sent back to a chosen destination when the form is submitted.

Creating forms

Two methods exist for creating forms:

- Using a **form template** from **Form Designer**, a purposely designed environment for creating and modifying forms. You can choose to keep the template as is or modify it to your requirements.

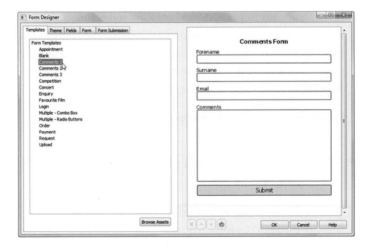

Form Templates are available for user appointments, comments, and login. Other popular forms that could be created from scratch by the user include CV submission forms and canvassing forms.

- Using an on-page **blank form** and adding form fields from the Quick Build tab.

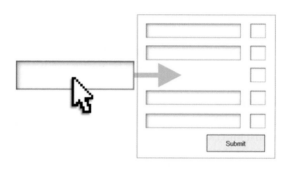

Creating forms (from a template)

The easiest way to create commonly used forms is to select one of the Form Designer's impressive range of form templates. These templates can be used without modification so they're almost ready to go—all you need to decide is where the submitted form data should be sent to. It's also easy to modify the template to your requirements by adding, deleting, or modifying individual fields.

To create a form using a template:

1. From the **Quick Build** tab, select ▦ **Form** from the Forms category and click on the page.

2. From the **Form Designer**, ensure the **Templates** tab is selected, then select a form template from the tab pane (e.g., Login, Appointment, etc.). Use the right-hand preview window to review each template.

3. From the **Theme** tab, select a specific look for your form.

4. (Optional) From the **Fields** tab (Add Field), click additional field to add them to your form. Delete unwanted fields or rearrange fields using the buttons under the preview page.

5. From the **Forms** tab, set a **Form Name**, **Form Title**, and **Width** for the form (not form fields).

6. From the **Form Submission** tab, choose a destination for your form data by clicking a destination button for email, or script file (local or remote), or **Serif Web Resources** and a name to define the whole form. (See **Submission of forms** on p. 131).

7. Click **OK**.

> If you haven't set up form submission, you'll be prompted to return to the Form Designer (by clicking Cancel) and set up how a user's form data is to be submitted. If you click OK, it's assumed that you'll set up form submission later.

The form is added to your page.

Customizing template forms

If you've selected a template form you can customize it to your own requirement. Form fields can be modified, reordered, or removed. Additional form fields can also be added.

To modify a field:

1. From **Form Designer** (**Templates** tab), double-click a form field in the right-hand preview pane.

2. Edit the **Field Properties** in the **Fields** tab. Options differ depending on the type of form field selected.

3. Use the default internal **Name** for the field (to uniquely identify it) or edit it, and then modify the **Label** to accompany the form field (this is shown on-screen).

To reorder fields:

- Select a form field in the preview window, then click **Move Up** or **Move Down**.

To remove a form field:

- Select a form field, and click **Delete**.

To add additional fields:

- Select the **Fields** tab (**Add Field**) and click the type of field you want to add.

> To add supporting text to your form (e.g., a competition question), you can click Text Label in the Advanced category.

For pre-populated combo boxes (such as Countries, UK Counties, US states, etc.), from the **Fields** tab, click **Assets** and select a combo box from the tab.

Creating forms (from scratch)

If you're looking for design freedom, WebPlus lets you create a blank
form directly on the page to which you can add form fields.

To create a blank form from scratch:

*   From the **Quick Build** tab, **Ctrl**-drag **Form** from the
    Forms category to the page.

The blank form, composed of a blank form area and a Submit button, is
added to the page. You can then add form fields to the form easily.

To add form fields to the form:

*   Click a form field, e.g. an Edit Box, on the Quick Build tab and
    then click in a form area to place the field.

Once form fields are positioned within the form, they are attached to it.
You can position the form and individual form fields using dynamic
guides, page guides or column/row guides like any other objects.

Forms as Assets

Some forms and form fields are assets, and as such belong to specific
asset packs. WebPlus lets you navigate from the Form Designer to your
Asset Browser and select an alternative form template (or form field) to
use.

You can also store any custom field or entire form to a custom asset
pack for future use. Fields can also be loaded from an Asset pack.

To access forms via the Asset Browser:

1. In **Form Designer** (**Templates** tab), click **Browse Assets**.

2. Select a form from the Asset Browser's **Page Content>Form Templates** category.

If you wish to store your own form field that you've modified from a template or created from scratch, it can be saved as an asset. See WebPlus Help.

Editing forms on the page

If you've created a form using a template it can be edited in Form Designer at any time. Forms created from scratch can be edited directly on the page.

To edit a template-based form:

1. Double-click the form.

2. In the Form Designer, select a form field for editing or apply a different theme from the **Theme** tab.

On the page, the form will always remain locked to prevent accidental editing. If you want to have form design freedom you can unlock it.

To unlock a template form for editing:

- From the Form context toolbar, select 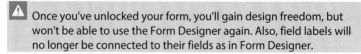 **Unlock Form**.

> ⚠ Once you've unlocked your form, you'll gain design freedom, but won't be able to use the Form Designer again. Also, field labels will no longer be connected to their fields as in Form Designer.

Unlocked forms and forms you create from scratch can be edited using normal object control in WebPlus. The form bounding box can be resized, pictures can be added to the form, the form can take a background colour (from the Colour tab), and form fields can be ordered and rearranged. Form field properties can also be edited independently of Form Designer.

To edit form fields:

- Double-click the form field.

Submission of forms

All forms have one thing in common—they must be submitted to allow data to be collected. This is done by the website visitor using a dedicated **Submit** button available as a form field when using **Form Designer** or when creating a form **from scratch**. The button needs to be present on the form and is typically used with a **Reset** button to clear all form fields of data.

Where is data sent?

After submission, form data can be sent to one of the following:

- **Serif Web Resources**; for transit of submitted form data to your email (via Serif).

- an email address (of the web developer).

- a script file (stored locally or remotely); this could write text to a text file or into a server database.

These submission options can be set up within Form Designer, using the Form Submission tab. Options have shared settings or settings independent of each other.

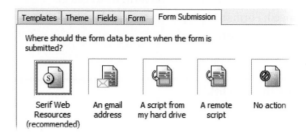

To set up Serif Web Resources submission:

1. With the **Serif Web Resources** icon enabled, click the **Select** button adjacent to the **Email Address** field (log in to Serif Web Resources if you're not already logged in).

2. From the dialog's Add new box, enter the target email address and click **Add new**.

    The email entry is created and added to the list. You'll notice that the entry is classed as Confirmed "No". Before the service commences, you'll get an email confirmation message sent to your email address. By clicking the link, the service will be activated and the entry will change to Confirmed "Yes".

    Click **Close**.

3. Back in Form Designer, select a **Target Window or Frame** in which a basic confirmation page is presented on submission. Select from the drop-down menu—if a Named Window or Document frame, the window/frame name can be specified. (See **Adding hyperlink and actions** on p. 56.)

4. Select a **Subject Field**. This sends the submitted form field data for a selected form field as the subject line of the email. Great for combo boxes, where emails can be easily sorted by subject line.

5. Check **Time Zone** and a city/region according to the website's location.

6. Select **Email Format** if the email is to be sent as plain text, HTML, or both. **Format** lets you set header text or footer text.

7. Check **Attach Data as Zip File** to bundle the submitted form data as a ZIP file, attached to the email.

8. Click **More Recipients** to add additional email addresses to send the form data to. These must already exist as form email targets.

9. Select the "Email" field from the **Confirmation Field** drop-down list if you want to automatically send an email confirmation back to the web visitor. (see below).

10. Click **OK**.

To protect against spam emails, Serif Web Resources uses a reCAPTCHA gateway if you haven't added a CAPTCHA or reCAPTCHA form field directly to your form. On form submission, this enables a security check offering a random text string for the web visitor to reproduce in a text box.

To set up an email address submission

Use the **email address** option to bypass the usual POST/GET submission methods. When the Submit button is pressed the web visitor's default email program is launched. The form data (passed in as a single string of text) is added to the email body and is ready to be sent to the configured email destination. Especially useful if there is no local or remote scripting in place.

This is an unsecure submission method—any private or confidential information will not be encrypted.

To set up email directly:

With the **A remote script** icon enabled, enter the destination **Email Address** (or select an already known email address from the drop-down list).

To set up a local script file:

The **A script from my hard drive** option is for experienced web developers with scripting expertise.

Navigate to and select your local script file, typically a .php, .js, .cfm, .cgi, .pl, .dll, or .exe file with the **Browse** button.

To set up a remote script file:

Use if your web host will not allow you to run your own scripts on your web space. Instead, your web host may supply a basic script file that can be linked to from your web page. Typically, the script will send the form data back to your email address (already setup with your web host).

1. With the icon opposite enabled, add a **Form name**.

2. Enter a URL pointing directly to a script file.

Choose a submission method, encoding type, target window/frame, and Character set.

To take no action:

Form data is not submitted. This option is useful if you want to temporarily disable data collection or if you haven't yet set up scripting or Serif Web Resources. At a later time you can edit the form (right-click then choose **Edit Form**) and select a valid submission method.

Importing text from a file

Importing text from a word-processor file is a quick way to build up text content for your site (but you can also create a story using WritePlus). If you use your current word processor (such as Microsoft Word) to create the text files for your site, you can import any number of files into one site.

WebPlus will import text into a selected **text frame** or create a new text frame if one is not selected. See **Inserting text frames** on p. 34 for more information.

> WebPlus will preserve the formatting of imported word-processor text. However, if you're using your word processor to create text specifically for WebPlus, you'll save time by typing as text only, and applying formatting later in WebPlus.

> Tables cannot be imported.

To import text into a new text frame:

1. Choose **Insert** > **Text File** from the **Text** menu.

2. From the **Insert Text File** dialog, select the format of the source file to be imported and locate the file itself.

3. Check the **Retain Format** box to retain the source file's formatting styles. Uncheck the box to discard this information. In either case, WebPlus will preserve basic character properties like italic, bold, and underline, and paragraph properties like alignment (left, centre, right, justified).

4. Click **Open**.

5. Drag out to place the text frame at your chosen dimensions.
    - or -

Click on the page or pasteboard to create a new frame at a default size.

You can also import text directly into a text frame which already exists on the page.

To import text into an existing frame:

1. If using an existing empty text frame, select the frame. If inserting text into a populated text frame, click for an insertion point (or select a portion of text to be replaced).

2. Follow steps 1-5 **above**.

    The text will be imported into the selected text object. For text frames, the text may overflow your frame. To resolve this, see **Controlling overflowing frame text** on p. 35.

Using artistic text

Artistic text is standalone text you type directly onto a page. Especially useful for headlines, pull quotes, and other special-purpose text, it's easily formatted with the standard text tools.

HAC HABITASSE

To create artistic text:

1. Choose the **A** **Artistic Text Tool** from the **Drawing** toolbar.

2. Click anywhere on the page for an insertion point using a default point size, or drag to specify a particular size as shown here.

3.   Set initial text properties (font, style, etc.) as needed before typing, using the Text context toolbar, **Text** menu, or right-click (choose **Text Format>**).

4.   Type directly on the page to create the artistic text.

Once you've created an artistic text object, you can select, move, resize, delete, and copy it just as you would with a text frame. Solid colours, gradient/bitmap fills and transparency can all be applied.

To resize or re-proportion an artistic text object:

•   Drag the object's corner handles to resize it while maintaining the object's proportions.

•   To resize freely, hold down the **Shift** key while dragging.

To edit artistic text:

•   Drag to select a range of text, creating a blue selection.

You can also double-click to select a word.

Now you can type new text, apply character and paragraph formatting, edit the text in WritePlus, apply proofing options, and so on.

Editing text on the page

You can use the Pointer Tool to edit **frame text**, **table text**, or **artistic text** directly. On the page, you can select and enter text, set paragraph indents and tab stops, change text properties, apply text styles, and use Find and Replace. For editing longer stories, and for more advanced options, choose WritePlus (**Edit Story** from the **Text** menu).

Selecting and entering text

The selection of frame text, artistic text, and table text follows the conventions of the most up-to-date word-processing tools. The selection area is shaded in semi-transparent blue for clear editing.

Nulla vestibulum eleifend
nulla. Suspendisse potenti.
Aliquam turpis nisi, venenatis
non, accumsan nec, imperdiet
laoreet, lacus.

Double-, triple-, or quadruple-click selects a word, paragraph or all text, respectively. You can also make use of the **Ctrl**-click or drag for selection of non-adjacent words, and the **Shift** key for ranges of text.

To edit text on the page:

1. Select the **Pointer Tool**, then click (or drag) in the text object. A standard insertion point appears at the click position (see below).

- or -

Select a single word, paragraph or portion of text.

2. Type to insert new text or overwrite selected text, respectively.

Nulla vestibulum eleifend
nulla. Suspendisse potenti.
Aliquam turpis nisi, venenatis
non, accumsan nec, imperdiet
laoreet, lacus.

To start a new paragraph:

- Press **Enter**.

To start a new line within the same paragraph (using a "line break" or "soft return"):

- Press **Shift+Enter**.

To switch between insert mode and overwrite mode:

- Press the **Insert** key.

Copying, pasting and moving text

You can easily copy and paste text using standard commands; drag and drop of text is also supported.

 If you don't place an insertion point, the text can be pasted into a new text frame directly.

Assets for
Creativity

11

Using assets

An **asset** is a general term for any object or page element that can be
added to your page to enhance its appearance, increase efficiency, or
personalize your design. Assets range from graphics, backgrounds,
pictures, picture frames, **buttons**, **sliders/panels**, various settings, to
more complex page content and entire **pages**.

To use assets, WebPlus provides the **Assets tab**, powered by both an
Asset Browser and Asset Manager (p. 144 and WebPlus Help,
respectively). The former browses your assets, the latter lets you create
and manage custom Asset Packs.

 Theme Layout design templates come complete with their own
built-in assets, all themed to the site's design. When you start from a
theme layout the **Assets** tab will be populated with associated
assets automatically!

Using the Assets tab

The **Assets** tab is a powerful design resource that exclusively hosts your browsed assets, ready for adding to your web page.

The tab also lets you save your own page objects for reuse globally or for use just in your site (by dragging to the My Designs category or dragging to another tab's category respectively). Settings, rather than actual objects, can be saved exclusively to the tab's Settings category.

See **Storing custom assets and asset settings** (p. 149).

Browsing for assets

Although initially empty, the tab can be populated with pre-designed assets by using an Asset Browser.

The Asset Browser

The Asset Browser lets you browse by asset category and Asset Pack (Pack Files), as well as search (by tag) for assets. Once displayed, the asset can be selected for inclusion in the **Assets** tab. See **Asset browsing** (p. 144) for more information.

The Asset Manager

Use the **Asset Manager** to create your own Asset Packs by using assets from other Asset Packs and/or by importing pictures, graphics, or PagePlus pack files. You can tag assets and then save or export your custom asset pack. (See WebPlus Help for details.)

Asset browsing

The **Asset Browser** offers a whole range of professional ready-to-go designs, called assets, that you can use directly in your site. These designs are provided in categorized pack files (also known as Asset Packs), installed with WebPlus.

There are two ways to browse assets before adding assets to your workspace—by category or by pack file.

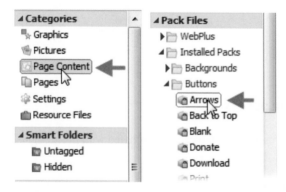

You can also use the search controls at the top-right of the dialog to narrow your search, or to find a specific assets in the pack files.

To browse assets (by category):

1.   From the **Assets** tab, click 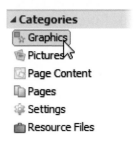 **Browse**.

2.   In the **Asset Browser**, select an asset category from the
     Categories section.

For example, for Graphics, you'll see available graphics appear
in sub-categories (e.g., Boxes, Flags, etc.) in the main pane.

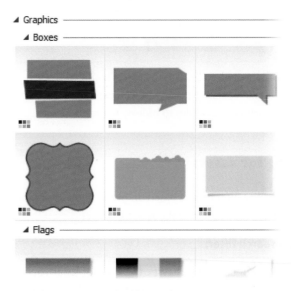

3.   Scroll through the sub-categories to browse and select additional assets.

To browse assets (by Pack File):

1. From the **Assets** tab, click 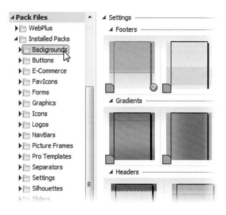 **Browse**.

2. In the **Asset Browser**, on the left-hand side of the dialog, select a pack file category (e.g., Backgrounds) or asset pack name from the **Pack Files** section. You may need to click the ▶ right arrow to expand a category for the latter. The pack file(s) will appear in the main pane.

3. Scroll through to browse the assets included in each pack file. To make browsing easier, you can expand and collapse the categories or pack files to hide or reveal the assets.

Searching for assets

The search facility filters assets based on preset and custom tags applied to all of the pack files shown in the **Asset Browser**.

To apply a search filter:

• For a simple tag search, type the word or letter you want to search for in the **Search** text box, situated at the top of the dialog. This is great for retrieving assets with custom tags.

> If your search results are being restricted to the currently highlighted category, Smart folder, Smart tag, or pack file, you can click the appropriate section header to remove this restriction.

Filtering assets

Filtering means that you can restrict the amount of assets on display.

- For **category** and/or **pack file filtering**, select a category or pack file (or multiple instances using **Ctrl**-click). You can also search for category and pack file combinations.

- For **Smart tag filtering**, select a tag name from the **Smart Tags** section (scroll down the left-hand pane). Smart tags let you filter assets logically by subject matter using a hierarchical and alphabetic tag structure. For example, if you select the "Wildlife & Nature" tag you'll see all assets tagged with that tag; if you want Animal-only assets, you could select "Animal", nested under that Occasions tag.

- For **tag-specific filtering**, select a tag name from the **Tags** section of the Asset Browser (below the Smart tags section). Use **Ctrl**-click to manually select multiple tags.

Adding assets to your Assets tab

To add a specific asset:

- Select the **category** or **pack file** in the Asset Browser, and then simply click the asset. A check mark shows on the thumbnail.

To add all assets:

- Click **Add All** from the upper-right corner of each Asset Pack's thumbnail gallery. Check marks will show on all thumbnails.

With either method, asset(s) will be available to you from the **Assets** tab when you close the Asset Browser.

To remove a specific asset (or all assets):

- From Asset Browser, click on the asset's thumbnail (or click **Remove All**).

  - or -

- From the **Assets** tab, click 🗑 **Remove** on the hovered-over thumbnail (or right-click **Select All**, then **Delete Assets**).

> Any asset stored in your **Assets** tab (but not added to the page) will be available to you the next time you open your site. Assets can be made globally available by **pinning** in the relevant tab category. Custom designs can also be made global by dragging page objects to the tab's My Designs category.

Adding assets to your page

To add an asset to the page:

- Click its thumbnail in the design category and drag it out onto the page.

Storing custom assets and asset settings

WebPlus lets you create and store custom assets from objects on the page; the settings of an object (its colour) can also be saved. This allows the assets to be used again either in your current WebPlus site or globally in any site in the future.

Objects and settings are added to the Assets tab by dragging from the page, then dragging back onto your page where (and when) you want it.

 Pages can't be dragged off your workspace but are added from within the tab category instead.

Storing to My Designs

If you're keen on storing your own objects for **global** use, the **Assets** tab's **My Designs** category is ideal—the stored assets will always be available in any new site you create.

When you first install WebPlus, the My Designs gallery will be empty, ready for objects to be added to it.

To store an object in My Designs:

- Drag the object from the page and drop it onto the **Assets** tab's My Designs category. You don't need to expand the category in advance, as it will automatically expand for you.

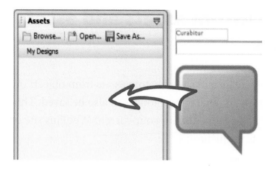

If you drag an object to any other category (or select pre-designed assets from Asset Packs within the Asset Browser), then the stored design will only be available to the current site.

Storing Pages

Any page already present in your site can be stored in the **Assets** tab (Pages category).

To store a page:

1. From the **Assets** tab's Pages category, click **Add**.

2. From the dialog, check a page (or master page) that exists in your site.

3. Click **OK**. The page appears in the Pages category.

Storing asset settings

Instead of storing an object, it's possible to store just an object's settings for reuse at a later date. As an example, a custom button's design could be saved, rather than the button itself.

Like storing objects, settings can be stored by drag and drop of the object, but to the Settings category only. A pop-up dialog lets you choose the type of settings needing to be saved.

Pinning categories and individual assets

Individual assets and entire categories within the **Assets** tab can be made available for all sites (i.e., globally) if they are pinned.

 Assets can only be pinned if they have been saved as part of an asset pack. If you attempt to pin an unsaved asset, you will be prompted to save your asset pack.

To pin and unpin assets:

- To pin all the assets in a category, click 📌 **Pin All** on the category header.

  - or -

  To pin an individual asset, click the 📌 icon on the individual asset.

- To unpin all the assets in a category, click 📌 **Unpin All** on the category header.

  - or -

  To unpin an individual asset, click the 📌 icon on the individual asset.

Previewing and Publishing

12

Tasks

The **Task Monitor** tab is used to report errors, problems, and reminders relating to your website prior to publishing. The task entries in the tab are interactive and let you resolve tasks automatically or manually.

At any time you publish, the tasks are displayed again in the publishing dialog—you can decide to proceed with publishing or be taken back to the Task Monitor tab to resolve tasks.

The tab is displayed at the bottom of the WebPlus workspace.

If tasks are found, the tab reports each task in a task list (showing Description, Due Date, Action, Object and Urgency) along with options to fix automatically or manually; you can also choose to leave some tasks as is. Each task has supporting help to aid you in resolving it.

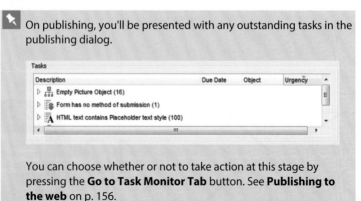

On publishing, you'll be presented with any outstanding tasks in the publishing dialog.

You can choose whether or not to take action at this stage by pressing the **Go to Task Monitor Tab** button. See **Publishing to the web** on p. 156.

Creating your own reminders

The Task Monitor tab allows you to create your own reminders that
need to be addressed before project completion. You can add reminder
text as well as set an urgency and a due date (e.g. a website go-live date).

Previewing your site

Previewing your site in a web browser is an essential step before
publishing it to the web. It's the only way you can see just how your site
will appear to a visitor. You can **preview** a page or site at any time, either
within WebPlus (using an internal window based on the Internet
Explorer browser) or separately using any browser installed on your
system.

To preview your site:

1. Click the down arrow on the ▦ ▾ **Preview site** button on the
   Standard toolbar.

2. Select an option from the submenu:

   • **Preview in Window** (shortcut **Alt+P**) opens the site in a
     new internal WebPlus window with its own tab.

   • Choose **Preview in** to use an external browser. The names
     will reflect which browsers are currently installed, e.g. the
     entry may read "Preview in Internet Explorer." The current
     page appears in the specified browser; use your page's
     navigation bars to navigate to other site pages.

▦ ▾ WebPlus allows you to view estimated download time for each
page of your site, and provides information such as the number of files
on each page and the total size of the files. This is carried out via the
Standard toolbar's **Preview site** flyout.

Publishing to the web (using WebPlus.net)

You can upload your site to WebPlus.net (Serif Web Hosting) so it's viewable by the whole world! You can specify that all web pages are published or, if updating your site, only pages changed since the last "publish."

To publish your site to WebPlus.net:

1.  Click the down arrow on the **Publish site** button on the **Standard** toolbar and click **Publish to Web**.

2. From the **Publish To Web: Get Hosting** dialog, click **Activate Now**.

Publish To Web: Get Hosting   ⬚

Before you publish your website, you need a web hosting account.

Set up Serif WebPlus.net hosting & a domain name.	Use existing hosting & domain name.	Publish your website later.
WebPlus.net hosting is the easiest and most convenient way to get your website live online – we'll even give you 30 days of free hosting. **It only takes a minute to set up and no technical expertise is required.**	If you already have your own WebPlus.net or third party hosting, just put the details into WebPlus to get your website online.	If you don't want to setup your hosting yet, you can do it later.
Activate Now	Add Details	Cancel

3. Follow the set up procedure on serif.com within your Internet browser. You'll be provided with a hosting page which contains FTP details you'll need to manually transfer to WebPlus.

4. In WebPlus's **Account Details** dialog, which popped up when you clicked **Activate Now**, transfer hosting details from your hosting setup page and paste them into the equivalent fields, e.g.

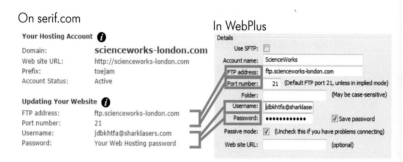

5. Click **OK** to close Account Details.

6. In the **Upload to server** dialog, click the **Test** button to test your FTP Account. If the test is successful, a dialog will display stating that a connection has been established.

7. Click **Update Account**.

The **Publish To Web** dialog can then be used to upload your website.

Publishing to the web (using a third-party host)

Publishing to the web using a third-party host involves uploading your site to a web host provider you've arranged independently of Serif.

To publish your site to the web:

1.   Click the down arrow on the **Publish site** button on the
   Standard toolbar and click **Publish to Web**.

   > If you haven't set up FTP account information, you'll be prompted to
   > add FTP details via a pop-up dialog.
   >
   > If you've set up at least one account, the **Publish to Web** dialog
   > appears with the last used account name shown in the drop-down
   > list and its settings in subsequent boxes.

2. From the **Publish To Web: Get Hosting** dialog, click **Add Details**.
    See screenshot on p. 156.

3. In the **Account Details** dialog, enter:

    • Check **Use SFTP** if your web host offers secure FTP
      connection. This protocol ensures data is securely transferred
      to your host using a private and safe data stream. Check your
      hosting package details to see if SFTP is included in your
      package.

    • The **Account name**. This can be any name of your choice.
      You'll use it to uniquely identify this account in WebPlus.

    • The **FTP address** of your web space—this is a specific URL that
      will be provided by your web host.

    • **Port number**: Unless directed by your provider, you can leave
      this set at "21."

    • Leave the **Folder** box blank unless directed by your provider, or
      if you want to publish to a subfolder of your root directory.

    • You'll also need a **Username** and **Password** as pre-assigned by
      the provider.

- Check **Save password** to record the password on your computer, if you don't want to re-enter it with each upload.

- **Passive mode**: Leave checked unless you are experiencing FTP connection problems.

  If you are certain that the FTP details are correct, unchecking **Passive mode** might fix the problem. ISPs and web hosts can operate passive or active FTP modes of operation, so it is worth checking this with them.

- **Web site URL**: Set your site's URL. This allows you to view the web site from a dialog after FTP upload.

- Click **OK** to close Account Details.

4. Back in the **Upload to server** dialog, click the **Test** button to test your FTP Account.

5. Click **Update Account**.

The **Publish To Web** dialog can then be used to upload your website.

Quick Publish

Quick Publish allows you to quickly upload and view the currently displayed page—useful for live verification of individual pages.

To configure Quick Publish:

1. Click the **Publish site** flyout on the **Standard** toolbar and then click **Quick Publish Configuration**.

2. In the dialog:

   - Enter the details of, or select from the drop-down list, the URL of the site you want to publish to.

   - Select the browser to view your page once it has been published.

   - Select the FTP account you want to use from the drop-down list. To update account settings, or add a new account, click **Manage Accounts**.

3. Click **OK**.

To Quick Publish to Web:

- Click the **Publish site** flyout on the **Standard** toolbar and then click **Quick Publish to Web**.

The **Uploading files** dialog briefly appears before your page is displayed in your chosen browser)

Additional
Information

13

Contacting Serif

Help with your Product

On the web	
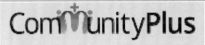	**community.serif.com** Get answers and ask questions in the Serif community!

Additional Serif information

On the web	
Serif website	**www.serif.com**

Main office	
Address	The Software Centre, PO Box 2000 Nottingham, NG11 7GW, UK
Phone	(0115) 914 2000
Phone (Registration)	(0800) 376 1989 +44 800 376 1989 800-794-6876 (US, Canada)
Phone (Sales)	(0800) 376 7070 +44 800 376 7070 800-489-6703 (US, Canada)
Customer Service	0845 345 6770 800-489-6720 (US, Canada)
Fax	(0115) 914 2020

Credits

This User Guide, and the software described in it, is furnished under an end user License Agreement, which is included with the product. The agreement specifies the permitted and prohibited uses.

Trademarks

Serif is a registered trademark of Serif (Europe) Ltd.

WebPlus is a registered trademark of Serif (Europe) Ltd.

All Serif product names are trademarks of Serif (Europe) Ltd.

Microsoft, Windows, and the Windows logo are registered trademarks of Microsoft Corporation. All other trademarks acknowledged.

Windows Vista and the Windows Vista Start button are trademarks or registered trademarks of Microsoft Corporation in the United States and/or other countries.

Google+ social service, Google Maps, Google Analytics web analytics service, and Google AdSense advertising service are trademarks of Google Inc.

Copyrights

Digital Images ©2008 Hemera Technologies Inc. All Rights Reserved.

Portions images ©1997-2002 Nova Development Corporation; ©1995 Expressions Computer Software; ©1996-98 CreatiCom, Inc.; ©1996 Cliptoart; ©1997 Multimedia Agency Corporation; ©1997-98 Seattle Support Group. Rights of all parties reserved.

This application was developed using LEADTOOLS, copyright © 1991-2007 LEAD Technologies, Inc. ALL Rights Reserved.

THE PROXIMITY HYPHENATION SYSTEM © 1989 Proximity Technology Inc. All rights reserved.

THE PROXIMITY/COLLINS DATABASE® © 1990 William Collins Sons & Co. Ltd.; © 1990 Proximity Technology Inc. All rights reserved.

THE PROXIMITY/MERRIAM-WEBSTER DATABASE® © 1990 Merriam-Webster Inc.; © 1990 Proximity Technology Inc. All rights reserved.

The Sentry Spelling-Checker Engine © 2000 Wintertree Software Inc.

The ThesDB Thesaurus Engine © 1993-97 Wintertree Software Inc.

WGrammar Grammar-Checker Engine © 1998 Wintertree Software Inc.

Andrei Stcherbatchenko, Ferdinand Prantl

PayPal © 1999-2012 PayPal. All rights reserved.

Roman Cart © 2008 Roman Interactive Ltd. All rights reserved.

Mal's © 1998 to 2003 Mal's e-commerce Ltd. All rights reserved.

iTunes © 2000 to 2008 Apple, Inc. All rights reserved.

YouTube © 2008 YouTube, LLC

TM + © 2013 Vimeo, LLC. All rights reserved.

Facebook © 2008 Facebook Inc.

Twitter © 2012 Twitter Inc.

phpBB © 2000, 2002, 2003, 2007 phpBB Group

FontForge © 2000,2001,2002,2003,2004,2005,2006,2007,2008 by George Williams.

Index

Notes

Notes

Notes